70 Brunch Recipes for Home

By: Kelly Johnson

Table of Contents

- Classic Eggs Benedict
- Avocado Toast with Poached Egg
- Smoked Salmon Bagel with Cream Cheese
- Blueberry Pancakes
- French Toast with Maple Syrup
- Breakfast Burritos
- Spinach and Feta Omelette
- Huevos Rancheros
- Shakshuka
- Quiche Lorraine
- Banana Walnut Muffins
- Greek Yogurt Parfait with Granola and Berries
- Chia Seed Pudding with Mango
- Breakfast Tacos with Salsa
- Croque Monsieur
- Breakfast BLT Sandwich
- Overnight Sausage and Egg Casserole
- Scones with Clotted Cream and Jam
- Veggie Breakfast Skillet
- Lemon Ricotta Pancakes
- Belgian Waffles with Fresh Berries
- Mushroom and Spinach Frittata
- Breakfast Quesadillas
- Crispy Hash Browns
- Quinoa Breakfast Bowl
- Apple Cinnamon French Toast Bake
- Caprese Avocado Toast
- Salmon Eggs Florentine
- Almond Butter and Banana Smoothie Bowl
- Baked Oatmeal with Berries
- Bagel Breakfast Sandwich
- Sweet Potato Hash with Fried Egg
- Cranberry Orange Scones
- Southwest Breakfast Wrap
- Raspberry Almond Coffee Cake

- Cinnamon Roll French Toast Casserole
- Pesto and Sun-Dried Tomato Quiche
- Grilled Cheese with Tomato Soup
- Chocolate Chip Pancakes
- Mediterranean Egg Salad
- Peanut Butter Banana Breakfast Wrap
- Breakfast Pizza with Eggs and Bacon
- Breakfast Stuffed Bell Peppers
- Lemon Poppy Seed Muffins
- Hawaiian Acai Bowl
- Tomato Basil Mozzarella Avocado Toast
- Prosciutto and Melon Bruschetta
- Biscuits and Gravy
- Spinach and Mushroom Breakfast Burritos
- Caramelized Onion and Goat Cheese Frittata
- Avocado and Bacon Breakfast Salad
- Blueberry Lemon Ricotta Pancakes
- Breakfast Sushi
- Strawberry Shortcake Waffles
- Quinoa and Black Bean Breakfast Bowl
- Pumpkin Spice Pancakes
- Breakfast Tostadas
- Cheddar and Chive Biscuits
- Corned Beef Hash
- Raspberry Chocolate Chip Muffins
- Spinach and Bacon Breakfast Wrap
- Caprese Omelette
- Banana Bread French Toast
- Mediterranean Avocado Toast
- Asparagus and Goat Cheese Frittata
- Mixed Berry Smoothie Bowl
- Chicken and Waffle Sliders
- Everything Bagel Breakfast Casserole
- Pineapple Coconut Chia Pudding
- Brunch Charcuterie Board

Classic Eggs Benedict

Ingredients:

For Hollandaise Sauce:

- 3 large egg yolks
- 1 tablespoon water
- 1 tablespoon lemon juice
- 1 cup unsalted butter, melted
- Salt and cayenne pepper to taste

For Eggs Benedict:

- 4 large eggs
- 4 English muffins, split and toasted
- 8 slices Canadian bacon or ham
- Fresh chives or parsley for garnish
- Salt and pepper to taste

Instructions:

Prepare Hollandaise Sauce:

In a heatproof bowl, whisk together the egg yolks, water, and lemon juice.
Create a double boiler by placing the bowl over a pot of simmering water (ensure the bottom of the bowl doesn't touch the water).
Whisk the egg yolk mixture constantly until it thickens slightly.
Gradually stream in the melted butter while continuing to whisk until the sauce has a smooth and velvety consistency.
Season the hollandaise sauce with salt and cayenne pepper to taste. Remove from heat and keep warm.

Poach the Eggs:

Fill a wide saucepan with water and bring it to a gentle simmer.
Crack each egg into a separate bowl.

Create a gentle vortex in the simmering water using a spoon and carefully slide the eggs, one at a time, into the center of the vortex.
Poach the eggs for about 3-4 minutes for a soft, runny yolk.
Remove the poached eggs with a slotted spoon and place them on a plate lined with a paper towel to absorb excess water.

Assemble Eggs Benedict:

Toast the English muffins halves and place them on serving plates.
Top each muffin half with a slice of Canadian bacon or ham.
Carefully place a poached egg on top of each Canadian bacon slice.
Spoon hollandaise sauce generously over each poached egg.
Garnish with fresh chives or parsley.
Season with salt and pepper to taste.

Serve immediately and enjoy this classic Eggs Benedict recipe for a delicious brunch!

Avocado Toast with Poached Egg

Ingredients:

- 2 slices of whole-grain bread
- 1 ripe avocado
- 2 large eggs
- Salt and pepper to taste
- Optional toppings: red pepper flakes, cherry tomatoes, feta cheese, or microgreens

Instructions:

Poach the Eggs:

Fill a wide saucepan with water and bring it to a gentle simmer.
Crack each egg into a separate bowl.
Create a gentle vortex in the simmering water using a spoon and carefully slide the eggs, one at a time, into the center of the vortex.
Poach the eggs for about 3-4 minutes for a soft, runny yolk.
Remove the poached eggs with a slotted spoon and place them on a plate lined with a paper towel to absorb excess water.

Prepare Avocado Toast:

Toast the slices of whole-grain bread to your liking.
While the bread is toasting, cut the ripe avocado in half, remove the pit, and scoop the avocado flesh into a bowl.
Mash the avocado with a fork and season it with salt and pepper to taste.
Spread the mashed avocado evenly over the toasted bread slices.

Assemble Avocado Toast:

Carefully place a poached egg on top of each avocado-covered toast.
Sprinkle additional salt and pepper on the eggs.
Add optional toppings like red pepper flakes, halved cherry tomatoes, crumbled feta cheese, or microgreens.

Serve immediately and enjoy this nutritious and delicious Avocado Toast with Poached Egg!

Smoked Salmon Bagel with Cream Cheese

Ingredients:

- 1 everything bagel, sliced and toasted
- 4 ounces smoked salmon
- 4 tablespoons cream cheese
- 1 tablespoon capers
- Red onion, thinly sliced
- Fresh dill, for garnish
- Lemon wedges, for serving

Instructions:

Prepare the Bagel:
- Toast the everything bagel slices to your liking.

Spread Cream Cheese:
- Spread a generous amount of cream cheese on each toasted bagel half.

Add Smoked Salmon:
- Arrange smoked salmon slices on top of the cream cheese.

Garnish with Toppings:
- Sprinkle capers over the smoked salmon.
- Add thinly sliced red onions for a zesty kick.

Finish with Fresh Dill:
- Garnish the bagel with fresh dill for a burst of flavor.

Serve with Lemon Wedges:
- Serve the smoked salmon bagel with lemon wedges on the side for a citrusy touch.

Enjoy:
- Serve immediately and savor the delightful combination of smoked salmon, creamy cheese, and fresh bagel flavors.

This Smoked Salmon Bagel with Cream Cheese makes for a classic and elegant breakfast or brunch option. Adjust the quantities of toppings according to your taste preferences.

Blueberry Pancakes

Ingredients:

- 1 cup all-purpose flour
- 2 tablespoons sugar
- 1 teaspoon baking powder
- 1/2 teaspoon baking soda
- 1/4 teaspoon salt
- 3/4 cup buttermilk
- 1/4 cup milk
- 1 large egg
- 2 tablespoons unsalted butter, melted
- 1 cup fresh or frozen blueberries

Instructions:

In a large mixing bowl, whisk together the flour, sugar, baking powder, baking soda, and salt.
In a separate bowl, whisk together the buttermilk, milk, egg, and melted butter.
Pour the wet ingredients into the dry ingredients and gently stir until just combined. Be careful not to overmix; it's okay if there are a few lumps.
Gently fold in the blueberries.
Preheat a griddle or a non-stick skillet over medium heat. Lightly grease with cooking spray or a small amount of butter.
Using a ladle or measuring cup, pour the pancake batter onto the hot griddle, forming circles.
Cook until bubbles form on the surface of the pancakes and the edges start to look set. Flip the pancakes and cook the other side until golden brown.
Remove the pancakes from the griddle and serve warm. You can top them with additional blueberries, maple syrup, whipped cream, or your favorite pancake toppings.

Enjoy your delicious blueberry pancakes!

French Toast with Maple Syrup

Ingredients:

- 4 slices of bread (thick slices work well)
- 2 large eggs
- 1/2 cup milk
- 1 teaspoon vanilla extract
- 1/2 teaspoon ground cinnamon
- Pinch of salt
- Butter for cooking
- Maple syrup for serving
- Optional toppings: powdered sugar, fresh berries, or whipped cream

Instructions:

In a shallow bowl, whisk together the eggs, milk, vanilla extract, ground cinnamon, and a pinch of salt.
Heat a griddle or a non-stick skillet over medium heat. Add a pat of butter to coat the surface.
Dip each slice of bread into the egg mixture, ensuring both sides are well-coated but not overly saturated.
Place the coated bread slices on the hot griddle or skillet. Cook for 2-3 minutes on each side or until they are golden brown and cooked through.
Remove the French toast from the griddle and transfer to serving plates.
Serve the French toast warm with maple syrup drizzled over the top. You can also add optional toppings like powdered sugar, fresh berries, or whipped cream.
Enjoy your delicious French toast with maple syrup!

Feel free to customize the recipe to your liking, and don't hesitate to experiment with different bread types or additional flavorings like nutmeg or orange zest.

Breakfast Burritos

Ingredients:

- 4 large flour tortillas
- 6 large eggs
- 1/4 cup milk
- Salt and pepper to taste
- 1 tablespoon cooking oil
- 1 cup cooked and diced breakfast sausage, bacon, or ham
- 1 cup shredded cheese (cheddar, Monterey Jack, or your favorite)
- Optional additions: diced tomatoes, bell peppers, onions, salsa, avocado, or sour cream

Instructions:

In a bowl, whisk together the eggs, milk, salt, and pepper.

Heat the cooking oil in a skillet over medium heat. Pour the egg mixture into the skillet and scramble the eggs until they are cooked through but still moist.

Warm the flour tortillas in a dry skillet or microwave for a few seconds.

Assemble the burritos by placing a portion of the scrambled eggs in the center of each tortilla.

Add the cooked and diced breakfast meat of your choice on top of the eggs.

Sprinkle shredded cheese over the eggs and meat.

Add any optional ingredients you like, such as diced tomatoes, bell peppers, onions, salsa, avocado, or sour cream.

Fold the sides of the tortilla inward, then roll it up tightly to create the burrito.

Repeat the process for the remaining tortillas.

Optionally, you can warm the assembled burritos in the skillet for a minute on each side to melt the cheese and give the tortilla a nice crispiness.

Serve the breakfast burritos warm and enjoy!

Feel free to customize the filling ingredients to suit your preferences, and don't hesitate to get creative with additional toppings or sauces. Breakfast burritos are easily adaptable to various dietary preferences and make for a quick and satisfying morning meal.

Spinach and Feta Omelette

Ingredients:

- 3 large eggs
- 1/4 cup milk
- Salt and pepper to taste
- 1 tablespoon butter or cooking oil
- 1 cup fresh spinach, chopped
- 1/4 cup crumbled feta cheese
- Optional: diced tomatoes, onions, or bell peppers for added flavor

Instructions:

In a bowl, whisk together the eggs, milk, salt, and pepper until well combined.
Heat the butter or cooking oil in a non-stick skillet over medium heat.
Add the chopped spinach to the skillet and sauté until wilted, about 1-2 minutes.
Pour the egg mixture over the spinach in the skillet.
Allow the eggs to set slightly at the edges. Using a spatula, gently lift the edges of the omelette, allowing the uncooked eggs to flow underneath.
When the eggs are mostly set but still slightly runny on top, sprinkle the crumbled feta cheese over one half of the omelette.
If desired, add diced tomatoes, onions, or bell peppers over the feta cheese.
Carefully fold the other half of the omelette over the filling, creating a half-moon shape.
Cook for an additional 1-2 minutes until the eggs are fully cooked, and the cheese is melted.
Slide the omelette onto a plate, and serve warm.

Feel free to garnish the omelette with additional feta cheese, fresh herbs, or a drizzle of hot sauce if you like. This spinach and feta omelette is a delicious and nutritious way to start your day!

Huevos Rancheros

Ingredients:

- 4 large eggs
- 4 corn tortillas
- 1 cup cooked and seasoned black beans (canned or cooked from dry)
- 1 cup salsa (store-bought or homemade)
- 1/2 cup shredded cheese (cheddar, Monterey Jack, or queso fresco)
- 1 avocado, sliced (optional)
- Fresh cilantro, chopped, for garnish
- Lime wedges, for serving

Instructions:

Warm the corn tortillas in a dry skillet or microwave for a few seconds until pliable.
In the same skillet, heat the black beans over medium heat until warmed through.
In another skillet, heat a small amount of oil over medium heat. Crack the eggs into the skillet and fry to your desired doneness.
Assemble the Huevos Rancheros: Place a warm tortilla on each plate. Spread a spoonful of black beans on top of each tortilla.
Place a fried egg on the beans on each tortilla.
Spoon salsa over the eggs. Sprinkle shredded cheese on top.
Optionally, garnish with avocado slices and chopped cilantro.
Serve the Huevos Rancheros immediately, with lime wedges on the side.

Feel free to customize this recipe by adding your favorite toppings, such as sliced jalapeños, sour cream, or hot sauce. Huevos Rancheros is a hearty and flavorful breakfast that brings a taste of Mexico to your table.

Shakshuka

Ingredients:

- 2 tablespoons olive oil
- 1 onion, finely chopped
- 1 bell pepper, diced (red or green)
- 2 cloves garlic, minced
- 1 teaspoon ground cumin
- 1 teaspoon sweet paprika
- 1/4 teaspoon cayenne pepper (adjust to taste)
- 1 can (28 ounces) crushed tomatoes
- Salt and pepper to taste
- 4-6 large eggs
- Fresh cilantro or parsley, chopped, for garnish

Instructions:

Heat olive oil in a large skillet or frying pan over medium heat.
Add the chopped onion and cook until softened, about 5 minutes.
Add the diced bell pepper and cook for an additional 3-4 minutes until the pepper begins to soften.
Stir in the minced garlic, ground cumin, sweet paprika, and cayenne pepper. Cook for 1-2 minutes until the spices are fragrant.
Pour in the crushed tomatoes and season with salt and pepper. Simmer the sauce for about 10-15 minutes, allowing it to thicken.
Make small indentations in the sauce with a spoon and carefully crack the eggs into the indentations.
Cover the skillet and let the eggs cook in the simmering sauce for 5-8 minutes or until the whites are set but the yolks are still runny (cook longer if you prefer firmer yolks).
Garnish with chopped cilantro or parsley.
Serve the Shakshuka directly from the skillet, either family-style or spooned onto individual plates.
Enjoy Shakshuka with crusty bread, pita, or your favorite bread for dipping.

Shakshuka is a comforting and flavorful dish that can be enjoyed for breakfast, brunch, or even dinner. It's a versatile recipe, and you can customize it by adding ingredients like feta cheese, olives, or spinach if you like.

Quiche Lorraine

Ingredients:

For the Pie Crust:

- 1 1/4 cups all-purpose flour
- 1/2 cup unsalted butter, cold and cubed
- 1/4 teaspoon salt
- 3-4 tablespoons ice water

For the Filling:

- 8 slices bacon, cooked and crumbled
- 1 cup shredded Gruyère or Swiss cheese
- 1 tablespoon all-purpose flour
- 1 cup heavy cream
- 4 large eggs
- Salt and black pepper to taste
- Pinch of nutmeg (optional)

Instructions:

Preheat the oven to 375°F (190°C).

Prepare the pie crust: In a food processor, combine the flour, cold butter, and salt. Pulse until the mixture resembles coarse crumbs. Add ice water, one tablespoon at a time, pulsing until the dough starts to come together.

Turn the dough out onto a floured surface and shape it into a disk. Wrap it in plastic wrap and refrigerate for at least 30 minutes.

Roll out the chilled dough on a floured surface to fit a 9-inch pie dish. Press the dough into the pie dish and trim the excess. Prick the bottom of the crust with a fork to prevent it from puffing up during baking.

Line the pie crust with parchment paper and fill it with pie weights or dried beans. Blind bake the crust for about 15 minutes. Remove the weights and parchment paper and bake for an additional 5 minutes until lightly golden.

In a bowl, toss the shredded cheese with 1 tablespoon of flour to coat.

In another bowl, whisk together the heavy cream, eggs, salt, black pepper, and nutmeg.
Sprinkle the crumbled bacon over the pre-baked pie crust, followed by the coated cheese.
Pour the egg and cream mixture over the bacon and cheese.
Bake the quiche in the preheated oven for 30-35 minutes or until the filling is set and the top is golden brown.
Allow the Quiche Lorraine to cool for a few minutes before slicing and serving.

Quiche Lorraine can be enjoyed warm or at room temperature. It makes for a delightful brunch or lunch option, and you can also experiment with additional ingredients like caramelized onions or sautéed mushrooms.

Banana Walnut Muffins

Ingredients:

- 2 to 3 ripe bananas, mashed
- 1/2 cup unsalted butter, melted
- 3/4 cup granulated sugar
- 1 large egg
- 1 teaspoon vanilla extract
- 1 1/2 cups all-purpose flour
- 1 teaspoon baking soda
- 1/4 teaspoon salt
- 1/2 teaspoon ground cinnamon
- 1/2 cup chopped walnuts

Instructions:

Preheat your oven to 350°F (175°C). Line a muffin tin with paper liners or grease the muffin cups.
In a large mixing bowl, mash the ripe bananas with a fork or potato masher.
In a separate bowl, melt the butter in the microwave or on the stovetop.
Add the melted butter to the mashed bananas and mix well.
Add the granulated sugar, egg, and vanilla extract to the banana-butter mixture. Mix until well combined.
In another bowl, whisk together the flour, baking soda, salt, and ground cinnamon.
Gradually add the dry ingredients to the wet ingredients, stirring until just combined. Do not overmix.
Fold in the chopped walnuts.
Spoon the batter into the prepared muffin cups, filling each about two-thirds full.
Optional: sprinkle a few extra chopped walnuts on top of each muffin for added texture.
Bake in the preheated oven for 18-20 minutes or until a toothpick inserted into the center of a muffin comes out clean.
Allow the banana walnut muffins to cool in the muffin tin for a few minutes before transferring them to a wire rack to cool completely.

Enjoy these banana walnut muffins as a tasty snack or breakfast treat. They are perfect with a cup of coffee or tea!

Greek Yogurt Parfait with Granola and Berries

Ingredients:

- 1 cup Greek yogurt (plain or flavored)
- 1/2 cup granola
- 1/2 cup mixed berries (strawberries, blueberries, raspberries, or any berries of your choice)
- 1 tablespoon honey or maple syrup (optional, for added sweetness)
- 1 tablespoon chopped nuts (such as almonds or walnuts) for garnish (optional)

Instructions:

In a glass or bowl, start by adding a layer of Greek yogurt.
Sprinkle a layer of granola over the yogurt.
Add a layer of mixed berries on top of the granola.
Repeat the layers until you fill the glass or bowl, finishing with a final layer of berries on top.
If desired, drizzle honey or maple syrup over the parfait for added sweetness.
Garnish with chopped nuts for extra crunch and flavor.
Serve the Greek yogurt parfait immediately and enjoy!

Feel free to customize your parfait by adding other ingredients such as chia seeds, coconut flakes, or a dollop of nut butter. The combination of creamy Greek yogurt, crunchy granola, and sweet-tart berries creates a well-balanced and satisfying treat that is not only delicious but also packed with protein and nutrients.

Chia Seed Pudding with Mango

Ingredients:

- 1/4 cup chia seeds
- 1 cup milk (dairy or plant-based like almond, coconut, or soy)
- 1-2 tablespoons honey or maple syrup (adjust to taste)
- 1/2 teaspoon vanilla extract
- 1 ripe mango, peeled, pitted, and diced

Instructions:

In a bowl, combine the chia seeds, milk, honey or maple syrup, and vanilla extract. Stir well to ensure the chia seeds are evenly distributed.

Cover the bowl and refrigerate the mixture for at least 2-3 hours, or preferably overnight. This allows the chia seeds to absorb the liquid and create a pudding-like consistency.

After the chia pudding has set, give it a good stir to break up any clumps and achieve a smooth texture.

In serving glasses or bowls, layer the chia pudding with diced mango. You can alternate between layers or simply place the mango on top.

Optionally, drizzle a bit of honey or maple syrup over the top for added sweetness.

Garnish with additional diced mango or other fresh fruits if desired.

Serve the chia seed pudding with mango immediately or refrigerate until ready to serve.

Chia seed pudding is not only delicious but also a great source of fiber, omega-3 fatty acids, and protein. The addition of sweet and juicy mango enhances the flavor, providing a tropical and satisfying treat. Feel free to experiment with different fruits, nuts, or seeds to create your own variations of this healthy and tasty dessert.

Breakfast Tacos with Salsa

Ingredients:

For the Breakfast Tacos:

- 4 small flour or corn tortillas
- 4 large eggs
- Salt and pepper to taste
- 1 tablespoon butter or cooking oil
- 1 cup cooked breakfast sausage or bacon, crumbled
- 1 cup shredded cheddar or Mexican blend cheese
- Optional toppings: sliced avocado, chopped cilantro, diced tomatoes, or sour cream

For the Salsa:

- 1 cup diced tomatoes
- 1/4 cup diced red onion
- 1/4 cup chopped fresh cilantro
- 1 tablespoon lime juice
- Salt and pepper to taste

Instructions:

Prepare the salsa by combining diced tomatoes, diced red onion, chopped cilantro, lime juice, salt, and pepper in a bowl. Mix well and set aside.
In a skillet, heat the butter or cooking oil over medium heat.
Crack the eggs into the skillet and scramble them until cooked to your liking. Season with salt and pepper.
Warm the tortillas in a dry skillet or microwave for a few seconds until pliable.
Assemble the breakfast tacos by dividing the scrambled eggs among the tortillas.
Top the eggs with crumbled breakfast sausage or bacon.
Sprinkle shredded cheese over the top.
Add your desired toppings, such as sliced avocado, chopped cilantro, diced tomatoes, or sour cream.
Spoon a generous amount of salsa over each breakfast taco.
Serve the breakfast tacos immediately, and enjoy!

Feel free to customize the breakfast tacos with your favorite ingredients and toppings. You can also add a dash of hot sauce or salsa verde for extra flavor. Breakfast tacos are a versatile and delicious way to kickstart your day.

Croque Monsieur

Ingredients:

For the Béchamel Sauce:

- 2 tablespoons unsalted butter
- 2 tablespoons all-purpose flour
- 1 cup milk
- Salt, pepper, and a pinch of nutmeg to taste

For the Croque Monsieur:

- 8 slices of good-quality bread (white or whole wheat)
- 8 slices of ham
- 1 1/2 cups shredded Gruyère or Emmental cheese
- Dijon mustard (optional)
- Butter for spreading

Instructions:

Preheat your oven to 400°F (200°C).
Start by making the béchamel sauce. In a saucepan, melt the butter over medium heat. Add the flour and whisk continuously for 1-2 minutes to form a roux.
Gradually whisk in the milk, ensuring there are no lumps. Continue cooking and whisking until the mixture thickens.
Season the béchamel sauce with salt, pepper, and a pinch of nutmeg. Remove from heat and set aside.
Lay out the slices of bread and spread a thin layer of Dijon mustard on half of them if desired.
Place a slice of ham on each mustard-covered slice.
Sprinkle a generous amount of shredded Gruyère or Emmental cheese over the ham.
Top each with another slice of bread to make a sandwich.
Generously spread butter on the outside of each sandwich.
Place the sandwiches on a baking sheet and bake in the preheated oven for about 10-15 minutes or until the tops are golden brown and the cheese is melted.

Once out of the oven, pour a spoonful of béchamel sauce over the top of each sandwich.
Serve the Croque Monsieur warm, and enjoy!

Croque Monsieur is often served as a warm and indulgent lunch or brunch dish. Pair it with a side salad for a complete meal. If you add a fried or poached egg on top, it becomes a Croque Madame.

Breakfast BLT Sandwich

Ingredients:

- 4 slices of bread (white, whole wheat, or your preference)
- 8 slices of bacon
- 4 large eggs
- 1 medium-sized tomato, sliced
- Lettuce leaves
- Mayonnaise
- Salt and pepper to taste
- Optional: Avocado slices or hot sauce for extra flavor

Instructions:

Cook the bacon in a skillet over medium heat until it reaches your desired level of crispiness. Remove from the skillet and drain on paper towels.
In the same skillet, cook the eggs to your preference (fried, scrambled, or poached). Season with salt and pepper.
Toast the slices of bread in a toaster or on a griddle until golden brown.
Spread mayonnaise on one side of each slice of bread.
Assemble the sandwiches: Place lettuce leaves on one slice of bread. Top with slices of tomato, cooked bacon, and the cooked egg.
If desired, add avocado slices or a dash of hot sauce for extra flavor.
Place another slice of bread with mayonnaise on top to complete the sandwich.
Repeat the process for the remaining sandwiches.
Cut the sandwiches in half diagonally, if desired, and serve immediately.

The Breakfast BLT Sandwich combines the classic elements of a BLT with the heartiness of eggs, making it a satisfying and delicious breakfast option. Feel free to customize it to your liking by adding other ingredients such as cheese or your favorite condiments.

Overnight Sausage and Egg Casserole

Ingredients:

- 1 pound breakfast sausage (pork or turkey), cooked and crumbled
- 8 slices bread, cubed
- 2 cups shredded cheddar cheese
- 1 1/2 cups milk
- 8 large eggs
- 1 teaspoon Dijon mustard
- 1/2 teaspoon salt
- 1/4 teaspoon black pepper
- Optional toppings: chopped green onions, diced tomatoes, or salsa

Instructions:

Grease a 9x13-inch baking dish.
In a large bowl, combine the cooked and crumbled sausage, cubed bread, and shredded cheddar cheese. Mix well.
In another bowl, whisk together the milk, eggs, Dijon mustard, salt, and black pepper.
Pour the egg mixture over the sausage, bread, and cheese mixture. Gently stir to ensure everything is evenly coated.
Pour the entire mixture into the greased baking dish, spreading it out evenly.
Cover the dish with plastic wrap and refrigerate overnight or for at least 4-6 hours.
When ready to bake, preheat the oven to 350°F (175°C).
Remove the casserole from the refrigerator and let it come to room temperature for about 15-20 minutes.
Bake in the preheated oven for 45-50 minutes or until the center is set and the top is golden brown.
Optional: Sprinkle chopped green onions, diced tomatoes, or salsa on top for additional flavor.
Allow the casserole to cool for a few minutes before slicing and serving.

This Overnight Sausage and Egg Casserole is perfect for feeding a crowd or for a fuss-free family breakfast. You can also customize it by adding vegetables like bell peppers or spinach for extra color and nutrition. Enjoy a hearty and delicious breakfast with minimal morning preparation!

Scones with Clotted Cream and Jam

Ingredients for Scones:

- 2 cups all-purpose flour
- 1/4 cup granulated sugar
- 1 tablespoon baking powder
- 1/2 teaspoon salt
- 1/2 cup unsalted butter, cold and cubed
- 2/3 cup milk
- 1 teaspoon vanilla extract
- 1 large egg (for egg wash)

For Serving:

- Clotted cream
- Strawberry jam or your favorite jam

Instructions:

Preheat your oven to 425°F (220°C). Line a baking sheet with parchment paper.
In a large bowl, whisk together the flour, sugar, baking powder, and salt.
Add the cold, cubed butter to the flour mixture. Using your fingers or a pastry cutter, work the butter into the flour until the mixture resembles coarse crumbs.
In a separate bowl, whisk together the milk and vanilla extract.
Pour the milk mixture into the flour mixture and stir until just combined. Do not overmix; the dough should be slightly sticky.
Turn the dough out onto a floured surface. Gently knead it a few times until it comes together.
Pat the dough into a circle about 1 inch (2.5 cm) thick. Use a round cutter (about 2 inches in diameter) to cut out the scones. Place the scones on the prepared baking sheet, leaving a little space between each.
In a small bowl, beat the egg and brush it over the tops of the scones to create a shiny finish.
Bake in the preheated oven for 12-15 minutes or until the scones are golden brown.
Allow the scones to cool on a wire rack.

To Serve:

- Split the cooled scones in half horizontally.
- Spread clotted cream generously on each half.
- Add a dollop of strawberry jam (or your favorite jam) on top of the clotted cream.
- Place the two halves back together, creating a scone sandwich.
- Serve and enjoy your scones with clotted cream and jam, preferably with a cup of tea.

This delightful combination of warm scones, rich clotted cream, and sweet jam is a timeless treat that is perfect for an elegant afternoon tea or a cozy breakfast.

Veggie Breakfast Skillet

Ingredients:

- 1 tablespoon olive oil
- 1 small onion, diced
- 1 bell pepper (any color), diced
- 1 zucchini, diced
- 1 cup cherry tomatoes, halved
- 2 cups baby spinach or kale, roughly chopped
- 4 large eggs
- Salt and pepper to taste
- Optional toppings: avocado slices, grated cheese, hot sauce, or fresh herbs

Instructions:

Heat olive oil in a large skillet over medium heat.
Add diced onion and bell pepper to the skillet. Sauté for 2-3 minutes until softened.
Add diced zucchini to the skillet and cook for an additional 2-3 minutes.
Stir in cherry tomatoes and cook until they start to soften and release their juices.
Add chopped spinach or kale to the skillet and cook until wilted.
Create small wells in the vegetable mixture and crack one egg into each well.
Season the eggs with salt and pepper.
Cover the skillet with a lid and cook until the eggs are cooked to your liking. If you prefer a runny yolk, it usually takes 3-4 minutes.
Optional: Sprinkle grated cheese on top of the skillet and cover until melted.
Remove from heat and garnish with avocado slices, fresh herbs, or a drizzle of hot sauce.
Serve the Veggie Breakfast Skillet directly from the skillet or transfer it to plates.

This Veggie Breakfast Skillet is not only delicious but also a versatile dish. Feel free to customize it by adding other vegetables like mushrooms, asparagus, or sweet potatoes. It's a great way to incorporate a variety of colorful and nutrient-rich vegetables into your morning routine.

Lemon Ricotta Pancakes

Ingredients:

- 1 cup all-purpose flour
- 2 tablespoons granulated sugar
- 1 teaspoon baking powder
- 1/2 teaspoon baking soda
- 1/4 teaspoon salt
- 1 cup ricotta cheese
- 3/4 cup milk
- 2 large eggs
- 1 tablespoon fresh lemon juice
- Zest of one lemon
- Butter or cooking oil for greasing the pan

Optional toppings:

- Fresh berries
- Maple syrup
- Powdered sugar

Instructions:

In a large bowl, whisk together the flour, sugar, baking powder, baking soda, and salt.
In a separate bowl, whisk together the ricotta cheese, milk, eggs, lemon juice, and lemon zest until well combined.
Pour the wet ingredients into the dry ingredients and gently stir until just combined. Do not overmix; some lumps are okay.
Preheat a griddle or non-stick skillet over medium heat. Grease with butter or cooking oil.
Scoop 1/4 cup portions of batter onto the griddle for each pancake. Cook until bubbles form on the surface, and the edges look set.
Flip the pancakes and cook the other side until golden brown.
Repeat the process until all the batter is used.
Serve the lemon ricotta pancakes warm with your favorite toppings, such as fresh berries, maple syrup, or a dusting of powdered sugar.

Enjoy these lemon ricotta pancakes for a delightful and flavorful breakfast or brunch. The combination of ricotta and lemon creates a light and fluffy texture with a hint of citrus that is sure to brighten your morning.

Belgian Waffles with Fresh Berries

Ingredients:

For the Belgian Waffles:

- 2 cups all-purpose flour
- 1 tablespoon sugar
- 1 tablespoon baking powder
- 1/2 teaspoon salt
- 1 3/4 cups milk
- 1/3 cup vegetable oil
- 2 large eggs
- 1 teaspoon vanilla extract

For Serving:

- Fresh berries (strawberries, blueberries, raspberries, or a mix)
- Maple syrup or honey
- Whipped cream (optional)

Instructions:

Preheat your Belgian waffle maker according to the manufacturer's instructions.
In a large bowl, whisk together the flour, sugar, baking powder, and salt.
In a separate bowl, whisk together the milk, vegetable oil, eggs, and vanilla extract.
Pour the wet ingredients into the dry ingredients and stir until just combined. It's okay if there are some lumps.
Grease the waffle maker with non-stick cooking spray or a light brushing of oil.
Pour the batter onto the center of the preheated waffle maker, spreading it evenly.
Close the waffle maker and cook according to the manufacturer's instructions, usually for about 4-5 minutes, until the waffles are golden brown and crisp.
Carefully remove the waffles and repeat the process with the remaining batter.
Serve the Belgian waffles warm, topped with a generous amount of fresh berries.
Drizzle maple syrup or honey over the waffles and berries.
Optionally, add a dollop of whipped cream for an extra indulgence.

Enjoy these Belgian waffles with fresh berries for a delicious and visually appealing breakfast or brunch. The combination of fluffy waffles and vibrant, juicy berries makes for a delightful treat that can be enjoyed on special occasions or whenever you want to elevate your morning meal.

Mushroom and Spinach Frittata

Ingredients:

- 8 large eggs
- 1/2 cup milk
- Salt and pepper to taste
- 1 tablespoon olive oil
- 1 small onion, finely chopped
- 8 ounces mushrooms, sliced
- 2 cups fresh spinach, roughly chopped
- 1 cup shredded cheese (cheddar, feta, or your choice)
- Optional: Fresh herbs (such as parsley or thyme) for garnish

Instructions:

Preheat your oven to 375°F (190°C).
In a bowl, whisk together the eggs, milk, salt, and pepper until well combined.
Heat olive oil in a large oven-safe skillet over medium heat.
Add the chopped onion to the skillet and sauté for 2-3 minutes until softened.
Add the sliced mushrooms to the skillet and cook for an additional 5-7 minutes until they release their moisture and become golden brown.
Add the chopped spinach to the skillet and cook for 1-2 minutes until wilted.
Spread the vegetables evenly in the skillet and pour the egg mixture over them.
Sprinkle the shredded cheese on top of the eggs.
Cook on the stovetop for 3-4 minutes, allowing the edges to set.
Transfer the skillet to the preheated oven and bake for 12-15 minutes or until the frittata is set and the top is lightly browned.
Remove the frittata from the oven and let it rest for a few minutes.
Garnish with fresh herbs, if desired.
Slice the frittata into wedges and serve warm.

This mushroom and spinach frittata is versatile, and you can customize it by adding other ingredients such as tomatoes, bell peppers, or different types of cheese. It's a great way to enjoy a wholesome and flavorful meal with the goodness of eggs and vegetables.

Breakfast Quesadillas

Ingredients:

- 4 large flour tortillas
- 1 cup cooked and crumbled breakfast sausage or bacon
- 4 large eggs, scrambled
- 1 cup shredded cheddar or Mexican blend cheese
- 1/2 cup diced bell peppers
- 1/4 cup chopped green onions
- Salt and pepper to taste
- Cooking oil or butter for cooking

Optional toppings:

- Salsa
- Sour cream
- Avocado slices
- Chopped cilantro

Instructions:

In a skillet over medium heat, cook the breakfast sausage or bacon until fully cooked. Remove from the skillet and set aside.
In the same skillet, add a little oil if needed and scramble the eggs. Season with salt and pepper to taste. Once cooked, set aside.
Wipe the skillet clean and place it back on medium heat.
Place a tortilla in the skillet and layer one side with shredded cheese.
Add a portion of the cooked sausage or bacon, scrambled eggs, diced bell peppers, and chopped green onions on top of the cheese.
Fold the tortilla in half over the filling, creating a half-moon shape.
Press down gently with a spatula and cook for 2-3 minutes on each side or until the tortilla is golden brown and the cheese is melted.
Repeat the process for the remaining tortillas and filling.
Once cooked, remove the quesadillas from the skillet and let them cool for a minute.
Slice each quesadilla into wedges and serve with your favorite toppings such as salsa, sour cream, avocado slices, or chopped cilantro.

Enjoy these breakfast quesadillas as a hearty and flavorful way to start your day. They are quick to make and can be customized based on your taste preferences.

Crispy Hash Browns

Ingredients:

- 4 large russet potatoes, peeled and grated
- 1 small onion, finely chopped (optional)
- 2 tablespoons all-purpose flour
- 1 teaspoon salt
- 1/2 teaspoon black pepper
- Vegetable oil or clarified butter for frying

Instructions:

Grate the peeled potatoes using a box grater or a food processor.
If using, finely chop the onion.
Place the grated potatoes (and chopped onion if using) in a clean kitchen towel or cheesecloth. Squeeze out as much moisture as possible from the potatoes.
In a large bowl, combine the grated potatoes, chopped onion, flour, salt, and black pepper. Mix well.
Heat a large skillet or griddle over medium-high heat and add enough vegetable oil or clarified butter to coat the bottom of the pan.
Once the oil is hot, take a handful of the potato mixture and press it down into a flat, compact patty. Place it onto the hot skillet.
Cook the hash browns for about 3-4 minutes on each side or until they are golden brown and crispy.
Use a spatula to flip the hash browns, being careful not to break them.
Repeat the process with the remaining potato mixture, working in batches if necessary.
Once cooked, transfer the hash browns to a paper towel-lined plate to absorb any excess oil.
Serve the crispy hash browns immediately with your favorite breakfast items.

Enjoy these homemade crispy hash browns as a side dish to your breakfast or brunch. They pair well with eggs, bacon, or sausage. Feel free to experiment with additional seasonings or add-ins to customize the flavor to your liking.

Quinoa Breakfast Bowl

Ingredients:

- 1 cup quinoa, rinsed
- 2 cups water or milk (dairy or plant-based)
- Pinch of salt
- 1 tablespoon honey or maple syrup (optional, for sweetness)
- Fresh fruit (such as berries, sliced banana, or diced mango)
- Nuts and seeds (such as almonds, chia seeds, or sunflower seeds)
- Greek yogurt or plant-based yogurt
- Drizzle of honey or maple syrup (optional, for extra sweetness)
- Additional toppings: shredded coconut, granola, or dried fruit

Instructions:

Rinse the quinoa under cold water.
In a saucepan, combine the rinsed quinoa, water or milk, and a pinch of salt.
Bring the mixture to a boil, then reduce the heat to low, cover, and simmer for about 15-20 minutes or until the quinoa is cooked and has absorbed the liquid.
Fluff the quinoa with a fork and sweeten with honey or maple syrup if desired.
Divide the cooked quinoa into serving bowls.
Top the quinoa with fresh fruit, nuts, and seeds.
Add a dollop of Greek yogurt or plant-based yogurt on top.
Drizzle with honey or maple syrup for extra sweetness if desired.
Customize your bowl with additional toppings like shredded coconut, granola, or dried fruit.
Serve the quinoa breakfast bowl immediately and enjoy!

This quinoa breakfast bowl is a well-balanced and wholesome meal that provides a mix of protein, fiber, and healthy fats. Feel free to get creative with your toppings to suit your taste preferences and nutritional needs.

Apple Cinnamon French Toast Bake

Ingredients:

- 1 loaf of French bread, cut into 1-inch cubes
- 4 large apples, peeled, cored, and sliced (e.g., Granny Smith or Honeycrisp)
- 6 large eggs
- 2 cups milk
- 1/2 cup heavy cream
- 1/2 cup granulated sugar
- 1/4 cup brown sugar
- 1 tablespoon vanilla extract
- 1 teaspoon ground cinnamon
- 1/4 teaspoon ground nutmeg
- Pinch of salt
- 1/2 cup chopped pecans or walnuts (optional)
- Maple syrup for serving

Instructions:

Grease a 9x13-inch baking dish.
Arrange the cubed French bread in the prepared baking dish.
In a large bowl, whisk together the eggs, milk, heavy cream, granulated sugar, brown sugar, vanilla extract, ground cinnamon, ground nutmeg, and a pinch of salt.
Pour the egg mixture over the cubed bread, making sure all the bread is well coated. Gently press the bread down with a spoon to ensure it absorbs the liquid.
Scatter the sliced apples over the top of the bread mixture.
If desired, sprinkle chopped pecans or walnuts over the apples.
Cover the baking dish with plastic wrap and refrigerate for at least 2 hours or overnight. This allows the bread to absorb the liquid.
Preheat your oven to 350°F (175°C).
Remove the plastic wrap from the baking dish and bake in the preheated oven for 45-50 minutes or until the top is golden brown, and the center is set.
Allow the French toast bake to cool for a few minutes before slicing and serving.
Serve warm with maple syrup.

This Apple Cinnamon French Toast Bake is a crowd-pleaser and perfect for special occasions or lazy weekend mornings. The combination of sweet apples, warm cinnamon, and custardy French toast is sure to make it a favorite.

Caprese Avocado Toast

Ingredients:

- 2 slices of your favorite bread (sourdough, whole grain, or artisanal)
- 1 ripe avocado
- 1 medium-sized tomato, sliced
- Fresh mozzarella cheese, sliced
- Fresh basil leaves
- Balsamic glaze or reduction
- Olive oil
- Salt and pepper to taste

Instructions:

Toast the slices of bread to your liking.
While the bread is toasting, mash the ripe avocado in a bowl. Add salt and pepper to taste.
Once the bread is toasted, spread a generous layer of mashed avocado onto each slice.
Arrange tomato slices on top of the mashed avocado.
Place slices of fresh mozzarella over the tomatoes.
Drizzle balsamic glaze or reduction over the mozzarella. If you don't have balsamic glaze, you can mix balsamic vinegar with a little honey and reduce it in a saucepan until thickened.
Garnish each toast with fresh basil leaves.
Finish with a drizzle of olive oil and a sprinkle of salt and pepper.
Serve immediately and enjoy your Caprese Avocado Toast!

This Caprese Avocado Toast combines creamy avocado, juicy tomatoes, fresh mozzarella, and aromatic basil, creating a delightful and flavorful open-faced sandwich.

It's a perfect breakfast or brunch option that's both satisfying and visually appealing.

Salmon Eggs Florentine

Ingredients:

- 4 large eggs
- 1 bunch fresh spinach, washed and trimmed
- 4 slices smoked salmon
- 2 English muffins, split and toasted
- Hollandaise sauce (homemade or store-bought)
- Salt and pepper to taste
- Chopped chives or fresh dill for garnish (optional)

Instructions:

Poach the eggs: Bring a pot of water to a simmer. Crack each egg into a separate small bowl. Create a gentle whirlpool in the simmering water using a spoon and carefully slide the eggs, one at a time, into the center of the whirlpool. Poach for about 3-4 minutes until the whites are set but the yolks remain runny. Use a slotted spoon to remove the poached eggs and place them on a plate lined with paper towels.

Saute the spinach: In a skillet over medium heat, sauté the fresh spinach until wilted. Season with salt and pepper to taste.

Assemble the dish: Place a slice of toasted English muffin on each plate. Top with a handful of sautéed spinach, a slice of smoked salmon, and a poached egg. Spoon hollandaise sauce generously over the poached eggs.

Garnish with chopped chives or fresh dill if desired.

Serve immediately and enjoy your Salmon Eggs Florentine!

This elegant and flavorful dish makes for a delicious breakfast or brunch option. The combination of poached eggs, smoked salmon, and hollandaise sauce creates a satisfying and luxurious meal.

Almond Butter and Banana Smoothie Bowl

Ingredients:

For the Smoothie Bowl:

- 2 ripe bananas, frozen
- 1/4 cup almond butter
- 1 cup almond milk (or any milk of your choice)
- 1 tablespoon chia seeds (optional, for added texture and nutrients)
- 1-2 tablespoons honey or maple syrup (optional, for sweetness)

Toppings:

- Sliced bananas
- Granola
- Sliced almonds
- Chia seeds
- Drizzle of almond butter
- Fresh berries or other fruits

Instructions:

In a blender, combine the frozen bananas, almond butter, almond milk, chia seeds (if using), and honey or maple syrup (if desired).
Blend until smooth and creamy. If the mixture is too thick, you can add more almond milk to achieve your preferred consistency.
Pour the smoothie into a bowl.
Top the smoothie bowl with sliced bananas, granola, sliced almonds, chia seeds, and any other desired toppings.
Drizzle a little more almond butter on top for extra flavor.
Serve immediately and enjoy your Almond Butter and Banana Smoothie Bowl!

Feel free to customize your smoothie bowl with additional toppings like shredded coconut, hemp seeds, or a sprinkle of cinnamon. Smoothie bowls are not only delicious but also a great way to incorporate a variety of nutrients into your morning routine.

Baked Oatmeal with Berries

Ingredients:

- 2 cups old-fashioned rolled oats
- 1/2 cup chopped nuts (such as almonds or walnuts) - optional
- 1/4 cup maple syrup or honey
- 1 teaspoon baking powder
- 1 teaspoon ground cinnamon
- 1/2 teaspoon salt
- 2 cups milk (dairy or plant-based)
- 2 large eggs
- 1/4 cup melted butter or coconut oil
- 2 teaspoons vanilla extract
- 2 cups mixed berries (strawberries, blueberries, raspberries)
- Additional berries for topping

Instructions:

Preheat your oven to 375°F (190°C). Grease a baking dish (approximately 9x9 inches).
In a large bowl, mix together the rolled oats, chopped nuts (if using), baking powder, ground cinnamon, and salt.
In a separate bowl, whisk together the maple syrup or honey, milk, eggs, melted butter or coconut oil, and vanilla extract.
Pour the wet ingredients into the bowl with the dry ingredients and mix until well combined.
Gently fold in the mixed berries.
Pour the mixture into the greased baking dish.
Bake in the preheated oven for 35-40 minutes or until the top is golden brown and the center is set.
Remove from the oven and let it cool for a few minutes.
Serve warm, topped with additional berries if desired.
Optionally, drizzle with more maple syrup or honey for extra sweetness.

Enjoy this Baked Oatmeal with Berries for a wholesome and flavorful breakfast. You can also customize it by adding your favorite nuts, seeds, or a dollop of yogurt on top. It's a perfect dish to make ahead for a convenient and nutritious morning meal.

Bagel Breakfast Sandwich

Ingredients:

- 1 bagel, sliced and toasted (your choice of flavor)
- 1 large egg
- 1 slice of cheese (cheddar, Swiss, or your preference)
- 2 slices of bacon or sausage patty (cooked)
- Salt and pepper to taste
- Optional toppings: sliced avocado, tomato, spinach, hot sauce, or condiments of your choice

Instructions:

Toast the bagel slices until golden brown.
Cook the egg to your liking. You can fry it, scramble it, or make it into a round shape using an egg ring.
Season the egg with salt and pepper during cooking.
If using bacon, cook it until crispy. If using a sausage patty, cook it according to the package instructions.
Place a slice of cheese on the bottom half of the toasted bagel.
Layer the cooked egg on top of the cheese.
Add the cooked bacon or sausage on top of the egg.
If desired, add additional toppings such as sliced avocado, tomato, spinach, or condiments of your choice.
Place the other half of the toasted bagel on top to complete the sandwich.
Press the sandwich gently to allow the cheese to melt.
Serve your Bagel Breakfast Sandwich warm and enjoy!

Feel free to get creative with your Bagel Breakfast Sandwich by incorporating different ingredients or trying various spreads. It's a versatile and customizable breakfast option that can be tailored to suit your taste preferences.

Sweet Potato Hash with Fried Egg

Ingredients:

- 1 large sweet potato, peeled and diced
- 1 small onion, finely chopped
- 1 red bell pepper, diced
- 2 tablespoons olive oil
- 1 teaspoon smoked paprika
- 1/2 teaspoon garlic powder
- Salt and pepper to taste
- 2-4 eggs
- Fresh parsley or chives for garnish (optional)

Instructions:

Heat olive oil in a large skillet over medium heat.
Add the diced sweet potatoes, chopped onion, and diced red bell pepper to the skillet.
Season with smoked paprika, garlic powder, salt, and pepper.
Cook the sweet potato hash mixture, stirring occasionally, until the sweet potatoes are tender and slightly crispy on the edges. This usually takes about 15-20 minutes.
While the sweet potato hash is cooking, prepare fried eggs in a separate pan. You can cook the eggs according to your preference, such as over easy, over medium, or sunny-side-up.
Once the sweet potato hash is cooked, divide it onto plates.
Top each portion with a fried egg.
Garnish with fresh parsley or chives if desired.
Serve the Sweet Potato Hash with Fried Egg immediately and enjoy!

This dish is not only delicious but also packed with nutrients from the sweet potatoes and eggs. It's a hearty and flavorful breakfast that can keep you energized throughout the morning. Feel free to customize it with additional toppings or spices based on your taste preferences.

Cranberry Orange Scones

Ingredients:

- 2 cups all-purpose flour
- 1/3 cup granulated sugar
- 1 tablespoon baking powder
- 1/2 teaspoon salt
- 1/2 cup unsalted butter, cold and cubed
- 1/2 cup dried cranberries
- Zest of one orange
- 2/3 cup heavy cream
- 1 large egg
- 1 teaspoon vanilla extract

For the Glaze:

- 1 cup powdered sugar
- 2 tablespoons fresh orange juice
- Zest of one orange

Instructions:

Preheat your oven to 400°F (200°C). Line a baking sheet with parchment paper.
In a large bowl, whisk together the flour, sugar, baking powder, and salt.
Add the cold, cubed butter to the flour mixture. Using your fingers or a pastry cutter, work the butter into the flour until the mixture resembles coarse crumbs.
Stir in the dried cranberries and orange zest.
In a separate bowl, whisk together the heavy cream, egg, and vanilla extract.
Pour the wet ingredients into the flour mixture and stir until just combined. Do not overmix; the dough should be slightly sticky.
Turn the dough out onto a floured surface. Gently knead it a few times until it comes together.
Pat the dough into a circle about 1 inch (2.5 cm) thick. Use a round cutter (about 2 inches in diameter) to cut out the scones. Place the scones on the prepared baking sheet, leaving a little space between each.
Bake in the preheated oven for 12-15 minutes or until the scones are golden brown.

While the scones are baking, prepare the glaze. In a bowl, whisk together powdered sugar, fresh orange juice, and orange zest until smooth.
Once the scones are baked and slightly cooled, drizzle the glaze over the top. Allow the glaze to set for a few minutes before serving.

Enjoy these Cranberry Orange Scones with a cup of tea or coffee for a delightful and flavorful treat. The combination of tart cranberries and citrusy orange makes them a perfect addition to your breakfast or brunch spread.

Southwest Breakfast Wrap

Ingredients:

- 4 large eggs
- Salt and pepper to taste
- 1 tablespoon olive oil
- 1/2 cup diced bell peppers (mix of colors)
- 1/2 cup diced red onion
- 1 cup black beans, drained and rinsed
- 1 teaspoon ground cumin
- 1 teaspoon chili powder
- 1/2 cup shredded cheddar or Monterey Jack cheese
- 4 large whole wheat or flour tortillas
- Salsa and sliced avocado for serving
- Fresh cilantro for garnish (optional)

Instructions:

In a bowl, whisk together the eggs and season with salt and pepper.

Heat olive oil in a skillet over medium heat.

Add diced bell peppers and red onion to the skillet. Sauté until softened, about 3-4 minutes.

Push the vegetables to one side of the skillet and pour the whisked eggs into the other side.

Scramble the eggs until fully cooked, mixing them with the sautéed vegetables.

Add black beans, ground cumin, and chili powder to the skillet. Stir to combine and heat through.

Sprinkle shredded cheese over the egg and vegetable mixture. Allow it to melt.

Warm the tortillas in a separate pan or microwave.

Divide the egg and vegetable mixture evenly among the tortillas.

Add a spoonful of salsa and a few slices of avocado to each wrap.

Garnish with fresh cilantro if desired.

Fold in the sides of the tortillas and roll them up to create the wraps.

Serve these Southwest Breakfast Wraps immediately, and enjoy a flavorful and

protein-packed breakfast with a southwestern twist. Feel free to customize the wraps with additional ingredients like diced tomatoes, sour cream, or hot sauce according to your taste preferences.

Raspberry Almond Coffee Cake

Ingredients:

For the Streusel Topping:

- 1/2 cup sliced almonds
- 1/4 cup granulated sugar
- 2 tablespoons all-purpose flour
- 2 tablespoons unsalted butter, melted

For the Coffee Cake Batter:

- 2 cups all-purpose flour
- 1 teaspoon baking powder
- 1/2 teaspoon baking soda
- 1/4 teaspoon salt
- 1/2 cup unsalted butter, softened
- 1 cup granulated sugar
- 2 large eggs
- 1 teaspoon almond extract
- 1 cup sour cream
- 1 1/2 cups fresh or frozen raspberries (if using frozen, do not thaw)

For the Glaze:

- 1/2 cup powdered sugar
- 1-2 tablespoons milk
- 1/2 teaspoon almond extract

Instructions:

Preheat your oven to 350°F (175°C). Grease and flour a 9-inch round cake pan.
Prepare the streusel topping: In a small bowl, combine sliced almonds, sugar, flour, and melted butter. Set aside.
In a medium bowl, whisk together flour, baking powder, baking soda, and salt. Set aside.
In a large bowl, cream together softened butter and sugar until light and fluffy. Add eggs one at a time, beating well after each addition. Stir in almond extract.

Gradually add the dry ingredients to the wet ingredients, alternating with the sour cream. Begin and end with the dry ingredients, mixing until just combined.
Gently fold in the raspberries.
Pour half of the batter into the prepared cake pan and spread it evenly.
Sprinkle half of the streusel topping over the batter.
Spoon the remaining batter over the streusel layer and smooth the top.
Sprinkle the remaining streusel topping over the batter.
Bake in the preheated oven for 45-50 minutes or until a toothpick inserted into the center comes out clean.
Allow the coffee cake to cool in the pan for 15 minutes, then transfer it to a wire rack to cool completely.
Prepare the glaze by whisking together powdered sugar, milk, and almond extract. Adjust the consistency by adding more milk if needed.
Drizzle the glaze over the cooled coffee cake.

Slice and enjoy your Raspberry Almond Coffee Cake with a hot cup of coffee or tea!

Cinnamon Roll French Toast Casserole

Ingredients:

For the Casserole:

- 2 tubes (12.4 oz each) refrigerated cinnamon rolls with icing
- 6 large eggs
- 1 cup milk (whole or any preferred type)
- 1 teaspoon vanilla extract
- 1 teaspoon ground cinnamon

For the Icing:

- Reserved icing from the cinnamon roll tubes
- 1/2 cup powdered sugar
- 2 tablespoons milk

Instructions:

Preheat your oven to 375°F (190°C). Grease a 9x13-inch baking dish.
Cut each cinnamon roll into quarters.
In a large bowl, whisk together the eggs, milk, vanilla extract, and ground cinnamon.
Place the quartered cinnamon rolls into the prepared baking dish.
Pour the egg mixture over the cinnamon rolls, making sure they are well-coated.
Gently press down on the cinnamon rolls to help them absorb the liquid.
Let the mixture sit for about 15 minutes to allow the cinnamon rolls to soak up the egg mixture.
Bake in the preheated oven for 25-30 minutes or until the top is golden brown and the center is set.
While the casserole is baking, prepare the icing. In a small bowl, combine the reserved icing from the cinnamon roll tubes, powdered sugar, and milk. Mix until smooth.
Once the casserole is done baking, remove it from the oven and let it cool for a few minutes.
Drizzle the icing over the warm casserole.
Slice and serve the Cinnamon Roll French Toast Casserole.

Enjoy this delicious and comforting breakfast casserole that combines the flavors of cinnamon rolls with the convenience of French toast. It's perfect for special occasions or whenever you want to treat yourself to a sweet and satisfying morning meal.

Pesto and Sun-Dried Tomato Quiche

Ingredients:

For the Pie Crust:

- 1 1/4 cups all-purpose flour
- 1/2 cup unsalted butter, cold and diced
- 1/4 teaspoon salt
- 3-4 tablespoons ice water

For the Filling:

- 1/2 cup basil pesto (store-bought or homemade)
- 1/2 cup sun-dried tomatoes, drained and chopped
- 1 cup shredded mozzarella cheese
- 1/2 cup grated Parmesan cheese
- 4 large eggs
- 1 cup heavy cream or whole milk
- Salt and pepper to taste
- Fresh basil for garnish (optional)

Instructions:

Preheat your oven to 375°F (190°C).
In a food processor, combine the flour, cold diced butter, and salt. Pulse until the mixture resembles coarse crumbs.
Gradually add ice water, one tablespoon at a time, and pulse until the dough comes together. Be careful not to overmix.
Turn the dough out onto a floured surface and gently knead it a few times to bring it together. Shape it into a disk, wrap in plastic wrap, and refrigerate for at least 30 minutes.
Roll out the chilled dough on a floured surface and fit it into a 9-inch pie dish. Trim the excess dough and crimp the edges.
Spread the basil pesto over the bottom of the pie crust.
Sprinkle the chopped sun-dried tomatoes over the pesto.

In a bowl, whisk together the eggs, heavy cream (or milk), mozzarella cheese, Parmesan cheese, salt, and pepper.
Pour the egg mixture over the pesto and sun-dried tomatoes in the pie crust.
Bake in the preheated oven for 35-40 minutes or until the quiche is set and the top is golden brown.
Allow the quiche to cool for a few minutes before slicing.
Garnish with fresh basil if desired.

Serve this Pesto and Sun-Dried Tomato Quiche warm or at room temperature. It's a delightful dish with a perfect balance of savory pesto, tangy sun-dried tomatoes, and cheesy goodness.

Grilled Cheese with Tomato Soup

Ingredients:

For the Grilled Cheese:

- 8 slices of your favorite bread (white, whole wheat, or sourdough)
- Butter, softened
- 8 slices of cheese (cheddar, Swiss, or your choice)

For the Tomato Soup:

- 2 tablespoons olive oil
- 1 onion, chopped
- 2 cloves garlic, minced
- 1 can (28 oz) crushed tomatoes
- 2 cups vegetable or chicken broth
- 1 teaspoon sugar
- 1 teaspoon dried basil
- 1/2 teaspoon dried oregano
- Salt and pepper to taste
- 1/2 cup heavy cream (optional, for a creamier soup)
- Fresh basil or parsley for garnish (optional)

Instructions:

For the Grilled Cheese:

> Butter one side of each slice of bread.
> Place a slice of cheese between two slices of bread, buttered side facing out.
> Heat a skillet or griddle over medium heat.
> Place the assembled sandwiches on the skillet and cook until the bread is golden brown and the cheese is melted, about 2-3 minutes per side.
> Remove from the skillet and let them rest for a minute before slicing.

For the Tomato Soup:

> In a large pot, heat olive oil over medium heat.
> Add chopped onions and cook until softened, about 3-4 minutes.
> Add minced garlic and cook for an additional 1-2 minutes until fragrant.

Pour in the crushed tomatoes and vegetable or chicken broth.
Stir in sugar, dried basil, dried oregano, salt, and pepper.
Bring the soup to a simmer and let it cook for about 15-20 minutes to allow the flavors to meld.
If using, stir in the heavy cream for a creamier soup. Adjust the seasoning to taste.
Use an immersion blender or transfer the soup to a blender to puree until smooth. Be cautious when blending hot soup.
Serve the Tomato Soup hot, garnished with fresh basil or parsley if desired.
Pair the Grilled Cheese sandwiches with the Tomato Soup and enjoy!

This classic duo is loved for its simplicity and comforting flavors. The warm, gooey grilled cheese complements the rich and tangy tomato soup perfectly. It's a timeless combination that's sure to satisfy your cravings.

Chocolate Chip Pancakes

Ingredients:

- 1 cup all-purpose flour
- 2 tablespoons granulated sugar
- 1 teaspoon baking powder
- 1/2 teaspoon baking soda
- 1/4 teaspoon salt
- 3/4 cup buttermilk
- 1 large egg
- 2 tablespoons unsalted butter, melted
- 1 teaspoon vanilla extract
- 1/2 cup chocolate chips
- Additional chocolate chips for topping (optional)
- Maple syrup or toppings of your choice

Instructions:

In a large bowl, whisk together the flour, sugar, baking powder, baking soda, and salt.
In a separate bowl, whisk together the buttermilk, egg, melted butter, and vanilla extract.
Pour the wet ingredients into the dry ingredients and gently mix until just combined. Do not overmix; it's okay if there are a few lumps.
Fold in the chocolate chips.
Heat a griddle or non-stick skillet over medium heat. Grease with a little butter or cooking spray.
Pour 1/4 cup of batter for each pancake onto the griddle.
If desired, sprinkle additional chocolate chips on top of each pancake.
Cook until bubbles form on the surface of the pancake and the edges look set, then flip and cook the other side until golden brown.
Continue until all the batter is used.
Serve the chocolate chip pancakes warm with your favorite toppings, such as maple syrup, whipped cream, or fresh berries.

Enjoy these fluffy and chocolatey pancakes for a delightful breakfast or brunch. They are sure to be a hit with chocolate lovers of all ages!

Mediterranean Egg Salad

Ingredients:

- 6 hard-boiled eggs, chopped
- 1/4 cup red onion, finely chopped
- 1/4 cup cucumber, diced
- 1/4 cup cherry tomatoes, halved
- 1/4 cup Kalamata olives, pitted and chopped
- 2 tablespoons feta cheese, crumbled
- 2 tablespoons fresh parsley, chopped
- 1 tablespoon fresh dill, chopped
- 1/4 cup Greek yogurt
- 2 tablespoons mayonnaise
- 1 tablespoon Dijon mustard
- Salt and pepper to taste

Instructions:

In a large bowl, combine the chopped hard-boiled eggs, red onion, cucumber, cherry tomatoes, Kalamata olives, feta cheese, parsley, and dill.
In a separate small bowl, mix together the Greek yogurt, mayonnaise, and Dijon mustard.
Add the yogurt mixture to the egg mixture and gently toss until everything is well coated.
Season the egg salad with salt and pepper to taste. Adjust the seasoning according to your preference.
Refrigerate the Mediterranean Egg Salad for at least 30 minutes to allow the flavors to meld.
Serve the egg salad on a bed of greens, as a sandwich filling, or with crackers.

Enjoy this Mediterranean-inspired egg salad that combines the richness of eggs with the fresh and tangy flavors of Mediterranean ingredients. It's a versatile and satisfying dish that's perfect for a light lunch or as a party appetizer.

Peanut Butter Banana Breakfast Wrap

Ingredients:

- 1 large tortilla (whole wheat or your preferred type)
- 2 tablespoons peanut butter (smooth or crunchy)
- 1 banana, peeled and sliced
- 1 tablespoon honey or maple syrup (optional)
- Granola or chopped nuts (optional, for added crunch)

Instructions:

Place the tortilla on a flat surface.
Spread the peanut butter evenly over the entire surface of the tortilla.
Arrange the banana slices in a single layer on top of the peanut butter.
Drizzle honey or maple syrup over the banana slices if you want some added sweetness.
Optionally, sprinkle granola or chopped nuts over the banana slices for extra crunch.
Starting from one edge, tightly roll up the tortilla, enclosing the banana and peanut butter filling.
If desired, you can slice the wrap in half diagonally for easier handling.
Enjoy your Peanut Butter Banana Breakfast Wrap immediately or wrap it in parchment paper for an on-the-go breakfast.

This breakfast wrap is not only delicious but also provides a good balance of carbohydrates, protein, and healthy fats to keep you fueled throughout the morning. Feel free to customize it with additional ingredients like chia seeds, shredded coconut, or a sprinkle of cinnamon based on your taste preferences.

Breakfast Pizza with Eggs and Bacon

Ingredients:

- 1 pizza dough (store-bought or homemade)
- Olive oil for brushing
- 1 cup shredded mozzarella cheese
- 1 cup cooked and crumbled bacon
- 4 large eggs
- Salt and pepper to taste
- Chopped fresh herbs (such as chives or parsley) for garnish

Instructions:

Preheat your oven according to the pizza dough package instructions or your homemade dough recipe.
Roll out the pizza dough on a floured surface to your desired thickness.
Transfer the rolled-out dough to a pizza stone or baking sheet lined with parchment paper.
Brush the surface of the dough with olive oil.
Sprinkle shredded mozzarella cheese evenly over the pizza dough.
Distribute the cooked and crumbled bacon over the cheese.
Create wells in the toppings for the eggs. Crack an egg into each well.
Season the eggs with a pinch of salt and pepper.
Bake in the preheated oven according to the pizza dough instructions or until the crust is golden and the eggs are cooked to your liking.
Once out of the oven, garnish with chopped fresh herbs.
Slice and serve the Breakfast Pizza with Eggs and Bacon.

Enjoy this savory and satisfying breakfast pizza that combines the goodness of eggs and bacon with the convenience of pizza. It's a crowd-pleaser and a great option for brunch or breakfast gatherings.

Breakfast Stuffed Bell Peppers

Ingredients:

- 4 large bell peppers, halved and seeds removed
- 8 large eggs
- Salt and pepper to taste
- 1 cup cooked breakfast sausage or bacon, crumbled
- 1 cup diced tomatoes
- 1 cup shredded cheddar or your favorite cheese
- Chopped fresh herbs (such as parsley or chives) for garnish
- Optional toppings: avocado slices, hot sauce, or salsa

Instructions:

Preheat your oven to 375°F (190°C).
Place the halved bell peppers in a baking dish, cut side up.
In a bowl, whisk together the eggs, salt, and pepper.
Pour the egg mixture into each bell pepper half, filling them about halfway.
Evenly distribute the crumbled breakfast sausage or bacon, diced tomatoes, and shredded cheese among the bell peppers.
Pour the remaining egg mixture over the fillings in each bell pepper.
Bake in the preheated oven for 25-30 minutes or until the eggs are set and the tops are golden brown.
Remove from the oven and let the stuffed bell peppers cool for a few minutes.
Garnish with chopped fresh herbs.
Serve the Breakfast Stuffed Bell Peppers with optional toppings like avocado slices, hot sauce, or salsa.

These stuffed bell peppers make for a protein-packed and vegetable-rich breakfast. They are not only delicious but also a visually appealing way to enjoy a balanced morning meal. Feel free to customize the fillings to suit your taste preferences.

Lemon Poppy Seed Muffins

Ingredients:

- 2 cups all-purpose flour
- 1 cup granulated sugar
- 2 tablespoons poppy seeds
- 2 teaspoons baking powder
- 1/2 teaspoon baking soda
- 1/4 teaspoon salt
- 1 cup plain yogurt
- 1/2 cup unsalted butter, melted and cooled
- 2 large eggs
- Zest of 2 lemons
- 2 tablespoons fresh lemon juice
- 1 teaspoon vanilla extract

For the Glaze:

- 1 cup powdered sugar
- 2-3 tablespoons fresh lemon juice

Instructions:

Preheat your oven to 375°F (190°C). Line a muffin tin with paper liners or grease the cups.
In a large bowl, whisk together the flour, sugar, poppy seeds, baking powder, baking soda, and salt.
In a separate bowl, whisk together the yogurt, melted butter, eggs, lemon zest, lemon juice, and vanilla extract.
Pour the wet ingredients into the dry ingredients and gently fold until just combined. Do not overmix; it's okay if there are a few lumps.
Divide the batter evenly among the muffin cups, filling each about 2/3 full.
Bake in the preheated oven for 18-20 minutes or until a toothpick inserted into the center comes out clean or with a few moist crumbs.
While the muffins are baking, prepare the glaze. In a bowl, whisk together powdered sugar and fresh lemon juice until smooth.

Allow the muffins to cool in the tin for a few minutes, then transfer them to a wire rack.
Drizzle the glaze over the warm muffins.
Let the glaze set for a few minutes before serving.

Enjoy these Lemon Poppy Seed Muffins with a cup of tea or coffee for a bright and citrusy treat. They are perfect for breakfast, brunch, or a sweet snack any time of the day.

Hawaiian Acai Bowl

Ingredients:

For the Acai Bowl Base:

- 2 packs of frozen acai puree (unsweetened)
- 1 frozen banana
- 1/2 cup frozen pineapple chunks
- 1/2 cup frozen mango chunks
- 1/2 cup coconut water or almond milk
- 1 tablespoon honey or agave syrup (optional, depending on sweetness preference)

Toppings:

- Granola
- Sliced banana
- Sliced strawberries
- Fresh pineapple chunks
- Shredded coconut
- Chia seeds
- Honey or agave syrup for drizzling

Instructions:

Remove the frozen acai puree packs from the freezer and let them thaw for a minute or two to make it easier to break apart.
Break the acai packs into chunks and place them in a blender.
Add the frozen banana, pineapple chunks, mango chunks, coconut water (or almond milk), and honey (if using) to the blender.
Blend until smooth and creamy. You may need to stop and scrape down the sides to ensure everything is well blended.
Pour the acai mixture into a bowl.
Arrange your desired toppings on the acai base. Use granola, sliced banana, sliced strawberries, fresh pineapple chunks, shredded coconut, chia seeds, and drizzle with honey or agave syrup.

Customize the toppings based on your preferences and the fruits you have on hand.

Serve immediately and enjoy your Hawaiian Acai Bowl with a spoon!

This Acai Bowl not only provides a burst of tropical flavors but also offers a variety of textures from the creamy acai base to the crunchy granola and fresh fruits. It's a perfect and vibrant breakfast or snack option.

Tomato Basil Mozzarella Avocado Toast

Ingredients:

- 2 slices of whole-grain bread (or your preferred bread)
- 1 ripe avocado, peeled and sliced
- 1-2 medium-sized tomatoes, sliced
- Fresh mozzarella cheese, sliced
- Fresh basil leaves
- Extra virgin olive oil
- Balsamic glaze (optional)
- Salt and pepper to taste

Instructions:

Toast the slices of bread to your desired level of crispiness.
While the bread is toasting, peel and slice the ripe avocado.
Once the bread is toasted, place the avocado slices on each slice of bread, mashing them slightly with a fork.
Arrange tomato slices on top of the mashed avocado.
Add fresh mozzarella slices over the tomatoes.
Place fresh basil leaves on top of the mozzarella.
Drizzle extra virgin olive oil over the toast.
If desired, add a touch of balsamic glaze for extra flavor.
Season with salt and pepper to taste.
Serve the Tomato Basil Mozzarella Avocado Toast immediately, and enjoy!

This avocado toast variation combines the creamy texture of avocado with the juicy tomatoes, fresh mozzarella, and aromatic basil. The addition of olive oil and balsamic glaze enhances the flavors, creating a delightful and satisfying breakfast or snack.

Prosciutto and Melon Bruschetta

Ingredients:

- Baguette or Italian bread, sliced
- Olive oil for brushing
- 1/2 cup ricotta cheese
- 1/2 teaspoon lemon zest
- 1 tablespoon fresh lemon juice
- Salt and pepper to taste
- Prosciutto slices
- Melon (cantaloupe or honeydew), thinly sliced
- Fresh mint leaves for garnish

Instructions:

Preheat your oven broiler or grill.
Brush the slices of baguette or Italian bread with olive oil.
Toast the bread slices under the broiler or on the grill until golden brown on both sides. Watch them closely to prevent burning.
In a bowl, mix ricotta cheese with lemon zest, lemon juice, salt, and pepper. Adjust the seasoning to taste.
Spread a generous layer of the ricotta mixture on each toasted bread slice.
Top each bruschetta with a slice of prosciutto, folding or arranging it to fit.
Add a thin slice of melon on top of the prosciutto.
Garnish each bruschetta with fresh mint leaves.
Arrange the Prosciutto and Melon Bruschetta on a serving platter.
Serve immediately and enjoy this delightful combination of sweet melon, creamy ricotta, and savory prosciutto.

This appetizer is perfect for summer gatherings or as a light and elegant snack. The contrasting flavors and textures create a harmonious and delicious bite that's sure to impress your guests.

Biscuits and Gravy

Ingredients:

For the Biscuits:

- 2 cups all-purpose flour
- 1 tablespoon baking powder
- 1 teaspoon sugar
- 1/2 teaspoon salt
- 1/2 cup unsalted butter, cold and diced
- 3/4 cup milk

For the Sausage Gravy:

- 1 pound ground pork sausage (mild or hot)
- 1/4 cup all-purpose flour
- 3 cups milk
- Salt and pepper to taste

Instructions:

Preheat your oven to 450°F (230°C).
In a large bowl, whisk together the flour, baking powder, sugar, and salt.
Add the cold, diced butter to the flour mixture. Using a pastry cutter or your fingers, work the butter into the flour until the mixture resembles coarse crumbs.
Pour in the milk and stir until just combined. Do not overmix; the dough should be slightly sticky.
Turn the dough out onto a floured surface. Gently knead it a few times until it comes together.
Pat the dough into a circle about 1 inch (2.5 cm) thick. Use a round cutter (about 2 inches in diameter) to cut out biscuits. Place the biscuits on a baking sheet, leaving a little space between each.
Bake in the preheated oven for 10-12 minutes or until the biscuits are golden brown.
While the biscuits are baking, cook the sausage in a skillet over medium heat, breaking it apart with a spoon as it cooks.

Once the sausage is browned, sprinkle the flour over it and stir to combine.
Gradually pour in the milk, stirring constantly to prevent lumps.
Continue cooking and stirring until the gravy thickens. Season with salt and pepper to taste.
Once the biscuits are done, split them in half and place them on serving plates.
Spoon the sausage gravy over the biscuits.
Serve immediately and enjoy your homemade Biscuits and Gravy.

This classic dish is hearty, savory, and perfect for a satisfying breakfast or brunch. It's a comforting Southern favorite that's sure to be a hit at the breakfast table.

Spinach and Mushroom Breakfast Burritos

Ingredients:

- 4 large flour tortillas
- 1 tablespoon olive oil
- 1 cup mushrooms, sliced
- 2 cups fresh spinach, chopped
- 1 bell pepper, diced
- 1 small onion, finely chopped
- 4 large eggs, beaten
- Salt and pepper to taste
- 1 cup shredded cheese (cheddar, Monterey Jack, or your choice)
- Salsa and sour cream for serving (optional)

Instructions:

In a large skillet, heat olive oil over medium heat.
Add chopped onions and bell pepper to the skillet. Sauté until softened, about 3-4 minutes.
Add sliced mushrooms to the skillet and cook until they release their moisture and become golden brown.
Add chopped spinach to the skillet and cook until wilted.
Push the vegetables to one side of the skillet and pour beaten eggs into the other side. Scramble the eggs until fully cooked.
Combine the scrambled eggs with the sautéed vegetables in the skillet. Season with salt and pepper to taste.
Warm the flour tortillas in a separate pan or microwave.
Divide the egg and vegetable mixture evenly among the tortillas.
Sprinkle shredded cheese over the filling.
Roll up each tortilla to form the burritos.
Optional: Heat the assembled burritos in a skillet for a few minutes to melt the cheese and crisp up the tortillas.
Serve the Spinach and Mushroom Breakfast Burritos with salsa and sour cream if desired.

These breakfast burritos are not only delicious but also packed with nutrients from the spinach and mushrooms. They can be customized with additional ingredients like diced tomatoes, avocado, or hot sauce according to your taste preferences. Enjoy these burritos as a hearty and satisfying breakfast or brunch option.

Caramelized Onion and Goat Cheese Frittata

Ingredients:

- 8 large eggs
- 1/4 cup milk or cream
- Salt and pepper to taste
- 2 tablespoons olive oil
- 2 large onions, thinly sliced
- 1 tablespoon butter
- 4 ounces goat cheese, crumbled
- Fresh thyme leaves for garnish (optional)

Instructions:

Preheat your oven to 375°F (190°C).
In a bowl, whisk together the eggs, milk or cream, salt, and pepper until well combined.
Heat olive oil in an oven-safe skillet over medium heat.
Add the sliced onions to the skillet and cook, stirring occasionally, until they become golden brown and caramelized. This may take about 15-20 minutes.
Once the onions are caramelized, add butter to the skillet and let it melt.
Pour the whisked egg mixture over the caramelized onions in the skillet.
Sprinkle crumbled goat cheese evenly over the eggs.
Cook on the stovetop for a few minutes, allowing the edges to set.
Transfer the skillet to the preheated oven and bake for 12-15 minutes or until the frittata is set in the center.
If you have a broiler, you can briefly broil the top for a golden finish.
Once cooked, remove the frittata from the oven, sprinkle fresh thyme leaves over the top (if using), and let it cool for a few minutes.
Slice and serve the Caramelized Onion and Goat Cheese Frittata warm.

This frittata is not only rich and savory but also has a beautiful combination of sweet caramelized onions and tangy goat cheese. It makes a lovely dish for a brunch gathering or a quick and satisfying meal.

Avocado and Bacon Breakfast Salad

Ingredients:

- 4 cups mixed salad greens (e.g., spinach, arugula, or your choice)
- 4 eggs
- 1 ripe avocado, sliced
- 6 slices bacon, cooked and crumbled
- 1 cup cherry tomatoes, halved
- 1/4 cup feta cheese, crumbled (optional)
- Salt and pepper to taste
- Olive oil and balsamic vinaigrette for dressing

Instructions:

In a large bowl, toss the mixed salad greens.
Heat a skillet over medium heat. Fry or poach the eggs to your liking.
Arrange the sliced avocado, crumbled bacon, and halved cherry tomatoes over the salad greens.
Place the cooked eggs on top of the salad.
If using, sprinkle crumbled feta cheese over the salad.
Season the salad with salt and pepper to taste.
Drizzle olive oil and balsamic vinaigrette over the salad for dressing.
Gently toss the salad to combine all the ingredients.
Serve the Avocado and Bacon Breakfast Salad immediately.

Enjoy this breakfast salad as a satisfying and nutritious way to start your day. The creamy avocado, crispy bacon, and runny eggs create a delicious combination of flavors and textures. Feel free to customize the salad with additional ingredients like nuts or seeds for extra crunch.

Blueberry Lemon Ricotta Pancakes

Ingredients:

- 1 cup all-purpose flour
- 1 tablespoon sugar
- 1 teaspoon baking powder
- 1/2 teaspoon baking soda
- 1/4 teaspoon salt
- 1 cup ricotta cheese
- 2 large eggs
- 1/2 cup milk
- Zest of 1 lemon
- Juice of 1 lemon
- 1 cup fresh or frozen blueberries
- Butter or oil for cooking
- Maple syrup for serving

Instructions:

In a large mixing bowl, whisk together the flour, sugar, baking powder, baking soda, and salt.
In a separate bowl, whisk together the ricotta cheese, eggs, and milk until well combined.
Add the lemon zest and lemon juice to the wet ingredients and mix again.
Pour the wet ingredients into the dry ingredients and gently stir until just combined. Be careful not to overmix; it's okay if there are a few lumps.
Gently fold in the blueberries.
Heat a griddle or non-stick skillet over medium heat and add a small amount of butter or oil.
Pour 1/4 cup of batter for each pancake onto the griddle.
Cook until bubbles form on the surface of the pancakes and the edges look set, then flip and cook the other side until golden brown.
Repeat until all the batter is used.
Serve the Blueberry Lemon Ricotta Pancakes warm with maple syrup.

These pancakes are light, fluffy, and bursting with the sweet-tart flavor of blueberries and the zesty freshness of lemon. The ricotta adds a creamy texture, making them a delightful breakfast or brunch option.

Breakfast Sushi

Ingredients:

- 2 cups cooked sushi rice, seasoned with rice vinegar and sugar
- 4 sheets of nori (seaweed)
- 4 eggs, scrambled
- 1 avocado, sliced
- Smoked salmon or cooked bacon strips
- Soy sauce and/or teriyaki sauce for dipping
- Sesame seeds for garnish (optional)
- Chopped green onions for garnish (optional)

Instructions:

Prepare the sushi rice according to the package instructions and season it with a mixture of rice vinegar and sugar while it's still warm. Let it cool to room temperature.
Cook the scrambled eggs until they are just set. You can season them with salt and pepper.
Lay a sheet of plastic wrap on a clean surface.
Place a sheet of nori on the plastic wrap.
Wet your hands with water to prevent sticking, and spread a thin layer of sushi rice over the nori, leaving a small border along the top edge.
Arrange a strip of scrambled eggs, avocado slices, and smoked salmon or bacon strips across the bottom edge of the rice.
Using the plastic wrap as a guide, tightly roll the nori and rice over the fillings, sealing the edge with a little water.
Repeat the process with the remaining nori sheets and fillings.
Once rolled, use a sharp knife to slice the roll into bite-sized pieces, like sushi.
Arrange the Breakfast Sushi pieces on a plate.
Optional: Drizzle with soy sauce or teriyaki sauce, and sprinkle with sesame seeds and chopped green onions for garnish.
Serve immediately and enjoy your Breakfast Sushi!

Feel free to customize the fillings based on your preferences. Other ideas include adding cream cheese, cucumber, or any of your favorite breakfast ingredients. Breakfast Sushi is a fun and visually appealing way to switch up your morning routine.

Strawberry Shortcake Waffles

Ingredients:

For the Waffles:

- 2 cups all-purpose flour
- 1/4 cup granulated sugar
- 1 tablespoon baking powder
- 1/2 teaspoon salt
- 1 3/4 cups milk
- 1/3 cup vegetable oil
- 2 large eggs
- 1 teaspoon vanilla extract

For the Strawberry Topping:

- 2 cups fresh strawberries, hulled and sliced
- 2 tablespoons granulated sugar

For the Whipped Cream:

- 1 cup heavy cream
- 2 tablespoons powdered sugar
- 1 teaspoon vanilla extract

Instructions:

Preheat your waffle iron according to the manufacturer's instructions.
In a large bowl, whisk together the flour, sugar, baking powder, and salt.
In a separate bowl, whisk together the milk, vegetable oil, eggs, and vanilla extract.
Pour the wet ingredients into the dry ingredients and stir until just combined. Be careful not to overmix; it's okay if there are a few lumps.
Pour the batter onto the preheated waffle iron and cook according to the manufacturer's instructions until the waffles are golden brown and crisp.
While the waffles are cooking, prepare the strawberry topping by tossing the sliced strawberries with granulated sugar. Let them sit for a few minutes to release their juices.

In a separate bowl, whip the heavy cream until soft peaks form. Add the powdered sugar and vanilla extract, and continue whipping until stiff peaks form. Once the waffles are done, assemble by placing a waffle on a plate, topping it with a generous spoonful of strawberries, and finishing with a dollop of whipped cream.
Repeat the process for additional waffles.
Serve the Strawberry Shortcake Waffles immediately and enjoy!

These Strawberry Shortcake Waffles make for a delightful and indulgent breakfast or brunch. The combination of sweet strawberries, fluffy waffles, and luscious whipped cream creates a treat that's sure to be a hit.

Quinoa and Black Bean Breakfast Bowl

Ingredients:

- 1 cup cooked quinoa
- 1/2 cup black beans, drained and rinsed (canned or cooked)
- 1 avocado, sliced
- 1 cup cherry tomatoes, halved
- 2 poached or fried eggs
- Fresh cilantro, chopped, for garnish
- Salt and pepper to taste
- Optional toppings: salsa, hot sauce, lime wedges

Instructions:

Cook quinoa according to package instructions.
In a bowl, assemble the breakfast bowl by placing cooked quinoa at the base.
Add black beans, sliced avocado, and halved cherry tomatoes on top of the quinoa.
In a separate pan, poach or fry eggs to your liking.
Place the poached or fried eggs on the quinoa and vegetable mixture.
Season with salt and pepper to taste.
Garnish the bowl with chopped fresh cilantro.
Optional: Add toppings like salsa, hot sauce, or a squeeze of lime juice.
Serve the Quinoa and Black Bean Breakfast Bowl immediately and enjoy!

This breakfast bowl is not only delicious but also customizable based on your preferences. It provides a balance of protein, healthy fats, and fiber to keep you fueled throughout the morning. It's a great way to incorporate nutritious ingredients into your breakfast routine.

Pumpkin Spice Pancakes

Ingredients:

- 1 cup all-purpose flour
- 2 tablespoons brown sugar
- 1 teaspoon baking powder
- 1/2 teaspoon baking soda
- 1/2 teaspoon ground cinnamon
- 1/4 teaspoon ground nutmeg
- 1/4 teaspoon ground ginger
- 1/4 teaspoon salt
- 3/4 cup buttermilk
- 1/2 cup pumpkin puree
- 1 large egg
- 2 tablespoons unsalted butter, melted
- 1 teaspoon vanilla extract

Instructions:

In a large mixing bowl, whisk together the flour, brown sugar, baking powder, baking soda, cinnamon, nutmeg, ginger, and salt.
In a separate bowl, whisk together the buttermilk, pumpkin puree, egg, melted butter, and vanilla extract.
Pour the wet ingredients into the dry ingredients and stir until just combined. The batter may be slightly lumpy, but avoid overmixing.
Let the batter rest for a few minutes to allow the baking powder to activate.
Heat a griddle or non-stick skillet over medium heat. Lightly grease with butter or cooking spray.
Pour 1/4 cup portions of batter onto the griddle for each pancake.
Cook until bubbles form on the surface of the pancakes and the edges look set, then flip and cook the other side until golden brown.
Repeat with the remaining batter.
Serve the Pumpkin Spice Pancakes warm with your favorite toppings, such as maple syrup, whipped cream, or chopped nuts.

Enjoy these Pumpkin Spice Pancakes as a comforting and flavorful fall breakfast. They capture the essence of autumn with the warm spices and pumpkin flavor, making them a delightful treat for the season.

Breakfast Tostadas

Ingredients:

- 4 corn tortillas
- 1 tablespoon vegetable oil
- 4 large eggs
- Salt and pepper to taste
- 1 cup refried beans
- 1 cup diced tomatoes
- 1 avocado, sliced
- 1/2 cup shredded cheese (cheddar, Monterey Jack, or your choice)
- Salsa, for serving
- Fresh cilantro, chopped, for garnish (optional)
- Lime wedges, for serving

Instructions:

Preheat your oven to 375°F (190°C).
Brush both sides of each corn tortilla with vegetable oil.
Place the tortillas on a baking sheet and bake in the preheated oven for 8-10 minutes or until they become crispy.
While the tortillas are baking, heat the refried beans in a saucepan over medium heat until warmed through.
In a skillet, fry the eggs to your liking, seasoning them with salt and pepper.
Once the tortillas are crispy, spread a layer of refried beans on each tortilla.
Top each tostada with a fried egg, diced tomatoes, sliced avocado, and shredded cheese.
Optional: Place the assembled tostadas back in the oven for a couple of minutes to melt the cheese.
Garnish with chopped cilantro, if desired.
Serve the Breakfast Tostadas with salsa on the side and lime wedges for squeezing.

These Breakfast Tostadas offer a combination of textures and flavors, from the crispy tortillas to the creamy beans, eggs, and avocado. Feel free to customize the toppings based on your preferences, adding ingredients like sautéed veggies, sour cream, or hot sauce for an extra kick.

Cheddar and Chive Biscuits

Ingredients:

- 2 cups all-purpose flour
- 1 tablespoon baking powder
- 1/2 teaspoon baking soda
- 1/2 teaspoon salt
- 1/2 cup unsalted butter, cold and diced
- 1 cup sharp cheddar cheese, grated
- 2 tablespoons fresh chives, finely chopped
- 3/4 cup buttermilk

Instructions:

Preheat your oven to 450°F (230°C). Line a baking sheet with parchment paper.
In a large bowl, whisk together the flour, baking powder, baking soda, and salt.
Add the cold, diced butter to the flour mixture. Use a pastry cutter or your fingers to work the butter into the flour until the mixture resembles coarse crumbs.
Stir in the grated cheddar cheese and chopped chives.
Make a well in the center of the dry ingredients and pour in the buttermilk.
Gently mix the ingredients until just combined. The dough will be sticky.
Turn the dough out onto a floured surface. Gently knead it a few times until it comes together.
Pat the dough into a circle about 1 inch (2.5 cm) thick.
Use a round cutter (about 2 inches in diameter) to cut out biscuits. Place the biscuits on the prepared baking sheet, leaving a little space between each.
Bake in the preheated oven for 10-12 minutes or until the biscuits are golden brown on top.
Remove from the oven and let the biscuits cool on a wire rack for a few minutes.
Serve the Cheddar and Chive Biscuits warm and enjoy!

These biscuits are loaded with the savory goodness of sharp cheddar and the freshness of chives. They are perfect as a side dish for soups, stews, or as a tasty addition to any meal.

Corned Beef Hash

Ingredients:

- 2 cups cooked corned beef, diced
- 2 cups potatoes, peeled and diced
- 1 onion, finely chopped
- 1 red bell pepper, diced
- 2 tablespoons unsalted butter
- Salt and pepper to taste
- Optional: chopped fresh parsley for garnish
- Poached or fried eggs for serving

Instructions:

In a large skillet, melt the butter over medium heat.
Add the diced potatoes to the skillet and cook until they are golden brown and cooked through. This may take about 10-15 minutes.
Add the finely chopped onion and diced red bell pepper to the skillet. Cook until the vegetables are softened.
Stir in the diced corned beef and cook for an additional 5-7 minutes, allowing the flavors to meld.
Season the Corned Beef Hash with salt and pepper to taste. Adjust the seasoning as needed.
If desired, garnish with chopped fresh parsley for a burst of freshness.
Serve the Corned Beef Hash warm, either on its own or with poached or fried eggs on top.

Corned Beef Hash is a versatile dish that can be enjoyed on its own, with eggs, or as a side. It's a great way to use up leftover corned beef, making it a popular choice after holidays like St. Patrick's Day. Enjoy this comforting and flavorful meal for a hearty breakfast or brunch.

Raspberry Chocolate Chip Muffins

Ingredients:

- 2 cups all-purpose flour
- 1/2 cup granulated sugar
- 1/4 cup brown sugar, packed
- 2 teaspoons baking powder
- 1/2 teaspoon baking soda
- 1/4 teaspoon salt
- 1 cup buttermilk
- 1/2 cup unsalted butter, melted and cooled
- 2 large eggs
- 1 teaspoon vanilla extract
- 1 cup fresh or frozen raspberries
- 1/2 cup chocolate chips (dark, semi-sweet, or your preference)

Instructions:

Preheat your oven to 375°F (190°C). Line a muffin tin with paper liners or grease the cups.

In a large bowl, whisk together the flour, granulated sugar, brown sugar, baking powder, baking soda, and salt.

In a separate bowl, whisk together the buttermilk, melted butter, eggs, and vanilla extract.

Pour the wet ingredients into the dry ingredients and stir until just combined. Be careful not to overmix.

Gently fold in the raspberries and chocolate chips.

Spoon the batter into the prepared muffin tin, filling each cup about two-thirds full.

Bake in the preheated oven for 18-20 minutes or until a toothpick inserted into the center comes out clean.

Allow the muffins to cool in the tin for a few minutes, then transfer them to a wire rack to cool completely.

Once cooled, serve and enjoy your Raspberry Chocolate Chip Muffins!

These muffins are a perfect treat for breakfast, brunch, or a sweet snack. The combination of juicy raspberries and chocolate chips creates a delightful flavor contrast in each moist and tender muffin.

Spinach and Bacon Breakfast Wrap

Ingredients:

- 1 large whole wheat or spinach tortilla
- 2 large eggs
- Salt and pepper to taste
- 1 cup fresh spinach leaves
- 2 slices cooked bacon
- 1/4 cup shredded cheddar cheese
- Hot sauce or salsa for optional garnish

Instructions:

In a bowl, beat the eggs and season with salt and pepper to taste.
Heat a non-stick skillet over medium heat. Pour the beaten eggs into the skillet.
Scramble the eggs until they are fully cooked and fluffy.
Lay the tortilla on a flat surface.
Place the fresh spinach leaves in the center of the tortilla.
Add the scrambled eggs on top of the spinach.
Lay the cooked bacon slices over the eggs.
Sprinkle shredded cheddar cheese evenly over the filling.
Optional: Drizzle hot sauce or salsa for an extra kick.
Fold the sides of the tortilla inward and then roll it up tightly from the bottom to create the wrap.
Place the wrap seam-side down on a skillet or pan over medium heat to seal the edge and warm it through.
Once the wrap is heated, remove it from the skillet and slice it in half diagonally if desired.
Serve the Spinach and Bacon Breakfast Wrap immediately and enjoy!

This breakfast wrap combines the savory goodness of bacon, the freshness of spinach, and the creaminess of scrambled eggs for a flavorful and satisfying morning meal. Feel free to customize the ingredients to suit your taste preferences.

Caprese Omelette

Ingredients:

- 3 large eggs
- Salt and pepper to taste
- 1 tablespoon olive oil
- 1/2 cup cherry tomatoes, halved
- 1/2 cup fresh mozzarella cheese, diced
- Fresh basil leaves, chopped
- Balsamic glaze for drizzling (optional)

Instructions:

Crack the eggs into a bowl, season with salt and pepper, and whisk until well combined.
Heat olive oil in a non-stick skillet over medium heat.
Pour the beaten eggs into the skillet, swirling them around to ensure an even spread.
Allow the eggs to set at the edges. As the edges set, lift them with a spatula, tilting the skillet to let the uncooked eggs flow to the edges.
Once the omelette is mostly set but still slightly runny on top, add the halved cherry tomatoes, diced mozzarella, and chopped fresh basil on one side of the omelette.
Gently fold the other side of the omelette over the fillings, creating a half-moon shape.
Continue cooking for a minute or two until the cheese starts to melt.
Carefully slide the omelette onto a plate.
Drizzle with balsamic glaze if desired.
Serve the Caprese omelette warm and enjoy!

The Caprese omelette combines the classic flavors of tomatoes, fresh mozzarella, and basil, creating a light and flavorful breakfast. It's a perfect choice for those who enjoy the vibrant taste of a Caprese salad in a warm and comforting omelette.

Banana Bread French Toast

Ingredients:

For the Banana Bread:

- 2 to 3 ripe bananas, mashed
- 1/3 cup unsalted butter, melted
- 1 teaspoon vanilla extract
- 1 teaspoon baking soda
- Pinch of salt
- 3/4 cup granulated sugar
- 1 large egg, beaten
- 1 1/2 cups all-purpose flour

For the French Toast:

- Slices of your homemade banana bread (cooled)
- 2 large eggs
- 1/2 cup milk
- 1 teaspoon vanilla extract
- Butter or cooking spray for cooking
- Optional toppings: sliced bananas, maple syrup, whipped cream, or chopped nuts

Instructions:

Preheat your oven to 350°F (175°C). Grease and flour a loaf pan.
In a mixing bowl, mash the ripe bananas with a fork.
Add melted butter, vanilla extract, baking soda, pinch of salt, sugar, beaten egg, and flour to the mashed bananas. Mix until just combined.
Pour the banana bread batter into the prepared loaf pan.
Bake in the preheated oven for about 60-70 minutes or until a toothpick inserted into the center comes out clean.
Allow the banana bread to cool completely before slicing it into thick slices.
In a shallow dish, whisk together eggs, milk, and vanilla extract to create the French toast batter.
Heat a skillet or griddle over medium heat and add butter or use cooking spray.
Dip each slice of banana bread into the egg mixture, coating both sides.
Cook the slices on the skillet until golden brown on each side.

Repeat until all slices are cooked.
Serve the Banana Bread French Toast warm with your favorite toppings such as sliced bananas, maple syrup, whipped cream, or chopped nuts.

Enjoy the rich and comforting flavors of banana bread in a new form with this delightful Banana Bread French Toast. It's a perfect way to elevate your breakfast or brunch experience.

Mediterranean Avocado Toast

Ingredients:

- 1 slice whole-grain bread, toasted
- 1/2 ripe avocado
- 1 tablespoon feta cheese, crumbled
- 1 tablespoon Kalamata olives, chopped
- 1 tablespoon cherry tomatoes, diced
- Fresh basil leaves, chopped
- Extra virgin olive oil
- Salt and pepper to taste
- Optional: red pepper flakes for a bit of heat

Instructions:

   Toast a slice of whole-grain bread to your liking.
   While the bread is toasting, mash the ripe avocado in a bowl. Season with salt and pepper.
   Spread the mashed avocado evenly over the toasted bread.
   Sprinkle crumbled feta cheese over the avocado.
   Top with chopped Kalamata olives, diced cherry tomatoes, and fresh basil leaves.
   Drizzle extra virgin olive oil over the top.
   Optional: Add a pinch of red pepper flakes for a touch of heat.
   Serve the Mediterranean Avocado Toast immediately and enjoy!

This Mediterranean-inspired avocado toast combines creamy avocado with the salty tang of feta, the brininess of Kalamata olives, and the freshness of tomatoes and basil. It's a delicious and satisfying way to start your day or enjoy a light meal with vibrant Mediterranean flavors.

Asparagus and Goat Cheese Frittata

Ingredients:

- 8 large eggs
- 1/2 cup milk
- Salt and pepper to taste
- 1 tablespoon olive oil
- 1 bunch asparagus, trimmed and cut into bite-sized pieces
- 1/2 cup crumbled goat cheese
- 1/4 cup grated Parmesan cheese
- 2 tablespoons fresh chives, chopped

Instructions:

Preheat your oven to 350°F (175°C).
In a bowl, whisk together the eggs, milk, salt, and pepper until well combined.
Heat olive oil in an oven-safe skillet over medium heat.
Add the asparagus pieces to the skillet and sauté for about 3-5 minutes until they are slightly tender.
Pour the egg mixture over the asparagus in the skillet.
Sprinkle crumbled goat cheese, grated Parmesan, and chopped chives evenly over the eggs.
Cook on the stovetop for a couple of minutes, allowing the edges to set.
Transfer the skillet to the preheated oven and bake for 12-15 minutes or until the frittata is set in the center.
If you have a broiler, you can briefly broil the top for a golden finish.
Once cooked, remove the Asparagus and Goat Cheese Frittata from the oven, let it cool for a few minutes.
Slice and serve the frittata warm.

This Asparagus and Goat Cheese Frittata is not only visually appealing but also offers a delightful combination of fresh asparagus, creamy goat cheese, and the rich flavor of Parmesan. It's a versatile dish that can be enjoyed for breakfast, brunch, or any meal of the day.

Mixed Berry Smoothie Bowl

Ingredients:

For the Smoothie Base:

- 1 cup mixed berries (strawberries, blueberries, raspberries, blackberries)
- 1 frozen banana, sliced
- 1/2 cup plain Greek yogurt
- 1/2 cup almond milk or any milk of your choice
- 1 tablespoon honey or maple syrup (optional for sweetness)

Toppings:

- Sliced strawberries
- Blueberries
- Raspberries
- Granola
- Chia seeds
- Coconut flakes
- Drizzle of honey or agave syrup (optional)

Instructions:

In a blender, combine the mixed berries, frozen banana slices, Greek yogurt, and almond milk.
Blend until smooth and creamy. If the consistency is too thick, you can add more almond milk a little at a time until you reach your desired thickness.
Taste the smoothie and add honey or maple syrup if you prefer additional sweetness. Blend again to incorporate.
Pour the smoothie into a bowl.
Arrange your desired toppings on the smoothie surface. Sliced strawberries, blueberries, raspberries, granola, chia seeds, and coconut flakes work well.
Drizzle with honey or agave syrup for extra sweetness if desired.
Serve the Mixed Berry Smoothie Bowl immediately and enjoy!

Smoothie bowls are not only delicious but also customizable based on your preferences. They provide a refreshing and nutrient-packed breakfast or snack. Feel free to get creative with different berries and toppings to make it your own.

Chicken and Waffle Sliders

Ingredients:

For the Chicken:

- 1 pound boneless, skinless chicken tenders or breasts, cut into slider-sized pieces
- 1 cup buttermilk
- 1 cup all-purpose flour
- 1 teaspoon garlic powder
- 1 teaspoon onion powder
- 1/2 teaspoon paprika
- Salt and pepper to taste
- Vegetable oil for frying

For the Waffles:

- 1 cup all-purpose flour
- 1 tablespoon sugar
- 1 teaspoon baking powder
- 1/2 teaspoon baking soda
- 1/4 teaspoon salt
- 1 cup buttermilk
- 1 large egg
- 2 tablespoons unsalted butter, melted
- Cooking spray for waffle iron

For Assembly:

- Maple syrup for drizzling
- Optional toppings: coleslaw, pickles, hot sauce

Instructions:

Marinate the chicken: In a bowl, marinate the chicken pieces in buttermilk for at least 30 minutes or overnight in the refrigerator.

Prepare the waffle batter: In a separate bowl, whisk together the flour, sugar, baking powder, baking soda, and salt. In another bowl, whisk together buttermilk, egg, and melted butter. Pour the wet ingredients into the dry ingredients and stir until just combined.

Preheat your waffle iron and lightly coat it with cooking spray. Cook the waffles according to the manufacturer's instructions.

Bread and fry the chicken: In a shallow dish, mix together the flour, garlic powder, onion powder, paprika, salt, and pepper. Dredge each piece of chicken in the seasoned flour. Heat vegetable oil in a skillet over medium-high heat and fry the chicken until golden brown and cooked through (internal temperature of 165°F or 74°C). Drain on a paper towel.

Assemble the sliders: Place a piece of fried chicken on a mini waffle. Drizzle with maple syrup and add optional toppings like coleslaw, pickles, or hot sauce. Top with another mini waffle to create a slider.

Serve the Chicken and Waffle Sliders warm and enjoy!

These Chicken and Waffle Sliders are a perfect combination of sweet, savory, and crispy. They make a fantastic appetizer, brunch dish, or party food, offering a delightful twist on the classic chicken and waffles.

Everything Bagel Breakfast Casserole

Ingredients:

- 6-8 everything bagels, cut into bite-sized pieces
- 8 large eggs
- 2 cups milk
- 1 teaspoon Dijon mustard
- 1 teaspoon garlic powder
- Salt and pepper to taste
- 1 cup shredded cheddar cheese
- 1 cup diced ham or cooked sausage (optional)
- 1/4 cup chopped green onions
- Everything bagel seasoning (store-bought or homemade)
- Cream cheese for serving (optional)

Instructions:

Preheat your oven to 350°F (175°C). Grease a 9x13-inch baking dish.
Cut the everything bagels into bite-sized pieces and spread them evenly in the prepared baking dish.
In a bowl, whisk together the eggs, milk, Dijon mustard, garlic powder, salt, and pepper.
Pour the egg mixture over the bagel pieces, ensuring they are evenly coated.
Gently press down on the bagels to help them soak up the egg mixture.
Sprinkle shredded cheddar cheese over the top of the casserole.
If desired, add diced ham or cooked sausage evenly over the casserole.
Sprinkle chopped green onions and a generous amount of everything bagel seasoning over the top.
Cover the baking dish with foil and let it sit in the refrigerator for at least 30 minutes or overnight to allow the bagels to absorb the egg mixture.
Bake the casserole in the preheated oven for 45-55 minutes or until the center is set and the top is golden brown.
Allow the Everything Bagel Breakfast Casserole to cool for a few minutes before slicing.
Optional: Serve with a dollop of cream cheese on top.
Enjoy your Everything Bagel Breakfast Casserole warm!

This casserole is a flavorful twist on classic breakfast casseroles, featuring the beloved taste of everything bagels. It's perfect for brunch or feeding a crowd, and you can easily customize it with your favorite ingredients.

Pineapple Coconut Chia Pudding

Ingredients:

- 1 cup coconut milk
- 1 cup pineapple juice
- 1/4 cup chia seeds
- 1-2 tablespoons honey or maple syrup (optional, depending on your sweetness preference)
- 1/2 cup fresh pineapple chunks
- Shredded coconut for garnish (optional)

Instructions:

In a bowl, whisk together coconut milk, pineapple juice, and honey or maple syrup (if using).
Add chia seeds to the mixture and whisk well to combine.
Allow the mixture to sit for about 5-10 minutes, whisking again after a few minutes to prevent clumping.
Cover the bowl and refrigerate the chia pudding for at least 3 hours or overnight. The chia seeds will absorb the liquid and create a pudding-like consistency.
Before serving, stir the chia pudding to ensure an even texture.
When ready to serve, layer the chia pudding in glasses or jars with fresh pineapple chunks.
Optionally, garnish with shredded coconut on top.
Serve the Pineapple Coconut Chia Pudding chilled and enjoy!

This chia pudding is not only delicious but also packed with fiber, omega-3 fatty acids, and tropical flavors. It's a great make-ahead option for a quick and nutritious breakfast or snack. Feel free to customize the recipe with additional toppings like sliced bananas, kiwi, or mango for extra tropical goodness.

Brunch Charcuterie Board

Ingredients and Suggestions:

Cheeses:
- Brie
- Goat cheese
- Sharp cheddar
- Gouda
- Cream cheese with herbs
- Blue cheese

Cured Meats:
- Prosciutto
- Salami
- Smoked salmon
- Ham or turkey slices

Bread and Crackers:
- Baguette slices
- Croissants
- Multigrain crackers
- Pita bread or chips
- Grilled sourdough slices

Fresh Fruits:
- Berries (strawberries, blueberries, raspberries)
- Grapes
- Sliced melon (watermelon, cantaloupe)
- Figs or dates
- Apple or pear slices

Dried Fruits:
- Apricots
- Mango
- Pineapple

Nuts:
- Almonds
- Walnuts
- Pistachios

Spreads and Dips:
- Fruit preserves or jams

- Honey
- Fig or balsamic reduction
- Hummus
- Artichoke dip
- Olive tapenade

Extras:
- Olives (green and black)
- Cherry tomatoes
- Pickles or gherkins
- Caprese skewers (mozzarella, cherry tomatoes, basil)
- Deviled eggs

Sweets:
- Dark chocolate or chocolate-covered nuts
- Mini pastries
- Yogurt parfaits with granola and berries

Herbs and Garnishes:
- Fresh basil leaves
- Rosemary sprigs
- Edible flowers (optional)

Instructions:

Select a Serving Board:
- Choose a large wooden board, slate, or a decorative platter to arrange your items.

Place Cheeses and Meats:
- Start by placing a variety of cheeses and cured meats on the board. Consider folding or rolling slices of prosciutto for an elegant presentation.

Add Breads and Crackers:
- Arrange an assortment of bread and crackers around the cheeses and meats. You can toast or grill some bread for added texture.

Incorporate Fresh Fruits:
- Intersperse fresh fruits like berries, grapes, and melon slices throughout the board for a burst of color.

Include Dried Fruits and Nuts:
- Fill small bowls or scatter dried fruits and a selection of nuts around the board.

Arrange Spreads and Dips:

- Place small bowls of fruit preserves, honey, hummus, or other dips strategically on the board.

Add Extras and Savory Elements:
- Position olives, cherry tomatoes, pickles, caprese skewers, and deviled eggs to complement the flavors.

Incorporate Sweets:
- Integrate small portions of sweets like chocolate, pastries, or yogurt parfaits for a touch of indulgence.

Garnish with Herbs:
- Add sprigs of fresh herbs like basil or rosemary for an aromatic touch. Edible flowers can enhance the visual appeal.

Serve and Enjoy:
- Once the board is assembled, serve it to your guests, and encourage them to mix and match flavors.

Feel free to customize your Brunch Charcuterie Board based on your preferences and seasonal availability. It's a versatile and creative way to present a variety of brunch delights for everyone to enjoy.

www.ingramcontent.com/pod-product-compliance
Lightning Source LLC
LaVergne TN
LVHW081559060526
838201LV00054B/1969